W9-AEJ-434

"If you are looking for a resource that is kid-friendly and will jump-start your family devotions, this book is for you. Written in the trenches by a father who values his role as spiritual leader, these interactive vignettes will aid both dads and moms in their quest to instill spiritual truth into the lives of the people who matter the most—their children. *Smashed Tomatoes* fills a huge gap, providing parents (caregivers) with practical insights and object lessons that make spiritual truth come alive. One look and you'll be hooked!"

John R. Strubhar, Superintendent
Great Lakes District, Evangelical Free Church of America

"I shoulda', coulda', woulda' if I'da had some good help. Now help is at your fingertips. No more excuses—this is great stuff!"

Bob Murfin, Former Director
The Evangelical Child and Family Agency

"*Smashed Tomatoes* is an outstanding resource . . . creatively biblical and practical!"

Bradley Bacon, Senior Pastor
Bethel Community Church, Chicago, Illinois

"Talking to someone about family devotions usually stirs up about as much excitement as pulling weeds on a hot day. This is not the case with this book! . . . It is practical, interesting and definitely not boring. If you have given up on family devotions, take heart. Here are some of the best suggestions . . . to put you back on track."

Clifford R. Raad, Executive Director, Emeritus
Greater Chicago Sunday School Association

"Creatively and interactively employing common objects and life experiences as teaching tools, Tim offers a way to make family devotions both instructive and enjoyable."

Robert A. Vogel, Professor of Homiletics
Western Seminary, Portland, Oregon

SMASHED TOMATOES, BOTTLE ROCKETS . . .

Smashed Tomatoes, Bottle Rockets . . . and Other Outdoor Devotionals You Can Do with Your Kids

Tim Shoemaker

HORIZON BOOKS

CAMP HILL, PENNSYLVANIA

HORIZON BOOKS

A DIVISION OF CHRISTIAN PUBLICATIONS, INC.
3825 Hartzdale Drive, Camp Hill, PA 17011
www.cpi-horizon.com
www.christianpublications.com

Smashed Tomatoes, Bottle Rockets . . .
ISBN: 0-88965-188-4
LOC Catalog Card Number: 00-135124
© 2001 by Horizon Books
All rights reserved
Printed in the United States of America

01   02   03   04   05   5   4   3   2   1

Unless otherwise indicated,
Scripture taken from the HOLY BIBLE:
NEW INTERNATIONAL VERSION ®.
Copyright © 1973, 1978, 1984 by the
International Bible Society. Used by
permission of Zondervan Bible Publishers.

Dedicated to

My three sons . . . Andy, Mark and Luke.
These devotions were born out of my love for you and our God.

And to my parents, whose dedication to family devotions
as I was growing up impacts me still.

Contents

A Word to the Reluctant Owner of This Book

Let me guess—your wife bought this book for you. Or maybe it was a well-meaning friend or relative. I thought so! You probably figure it was their way of "encouraging" you to take the lead in the area of family devotions.

And you're also probably not too thrilled about the idea. Hey, I don't blame you. Only a dad who has tried and failed in the area of family devotions can really understand why you're so reluctant to jump into that shark pit again.

The way I see it, you have only two options. You can do nothing; you can stall it off. Most guys are pretty good at that when it comes to family devotions. Call it your form of protest if you like, but you can simply refuse to lead a family devotional time. Of course, if you do, it's still going to eat away at you. Deep down you'd like to be successful in this area. And if you don't make an effort, the person who gave you this book will have their hopes crushed.

The other option is to give this book a try. *Smashed Tomatoes, Bottle Rockets . . . and Other Outdoor Family Devotions You Can Do with Your Kids* is written *for* dads, *by* a dad. If you want the kids interested in family devotions, you need to get them involved. With boys especially, involvement means action. Each of the devotions in this book has just the right combination: an interest-catching activity with a ten-minute lesson built around it.

"Sounds great," you might be saying, "but how could I possibly prepare something like this every day?" Don't worry! The idea is to have family devotions *once a week* and really make them special. This book will cue you each week as to what you need to do to prepare. The lesson itself is written to you, the parent, and "coaches" you through each devotional time. It's easy. It's effective. It's fun. Maybe you could start out with one of the simpler ones, like "Smashed Tomatoes." Trust me; you can handle this!

I've been in your position. I avoided family devotions for years. I could make excuses to myself, but inside I didn't feel right about it. I'd start family "devoes," and then I'd stop. Every time I'd stop, the guilt inside grew. When I finally found a method that worked, I felt a whole lot better about myself. You will too.

Get ready for a shock: Your kids will enjoy them—even boys! Best of all, they are getting spiritual leadership from their dad, something they desperately need. And think how good you'll be feeling without that guilty spot in your heart!

One of the greatest truths I've ever heard is, "Sometimes you have to do something you don't like to protect something you love." Dads may not like the thought of family devotions, but we need to do it to protect the kids we love.

This book will be a tremendous help toward meaningful, fun family devotions. You may still have some tough moments, but it will get better. You can't expect to hit a home run every time you lead family devotions, but you're not always going to strike out, either. So stick with it—you may even begin to *like* family devotions!

"But I'm Not a Dad . . . I'm a Mom!"

Hey! There's no reason why moms can't use this book. Sure, it was designed for dads, but it works great for moms too!

The key is that the devotions work for the *kids*—even boys. Kids will enjoy the activities and object lessons built into these devoes.

It would be great if Dad were able to lead the family devotions. That isn't always possible. In those cases, *somebody* needs to do the job or the kids lose a perfect opportunity to learn important truths.

So don't worry if you aren't the dad. These devotions can also be led by Mom, Grandpa, Grandma or even Aunt Matilda!

How to Use This Book

Here are a few things to keep in mind as you start out:

1. *Keep your family devotional time short.* Most of the time there will be some kind of activity to do before you actually tie the devotional together with some real teaching. It's OK to extend the activity time if the kids are really enjoying it, but you want to keep your teaching time to about ten minutes. Less is more. This is extremely important. If you start going longer, you'll bore the kids. Once they're bored, your job gets a lot tougher. If you keep it short, the kids are less likely to tune you out.

2. *Plan ahead.* These family devoes are designed to be done once a week. The key is to do them well, and that takes a little bit of preparation. Read the devoes for the upcoming week well ahead of time. Sometimes you'll need to pick up some supplies or arrange for some help.

3. *Let the book be your guide.* The parts written in the shaded areas are just for you. That's where I play "coach" to help you through the devotional. And don't think you need to memorize the lesson, either. When I'm doing family devoes, I always have my notes in front of me, just like they're written in this book.

4. *Personalize the devotions.* Gear them to the age of your kids. The devoes in this book work pretty well for ages ten to fourteen. If your kids are older or younger you may need to make some adjustments. The rest comes down to preparation and persistence. As you read the devotional in advance, you may see some areas where you'd like to slip in a personal

example or one from the news that week. Excellent! That will make your devoes that much better.

5. *Don't let little problems discourage you.* OK, you *will* get discouraged from time to time, but keep going. It'll get better—trust me. If you miss a week, don't beat yourself up over it; just get back on track as soon as you can. If the kids don't seem to be paying attention, don't be fooled; they hear everything you say. Are they fooling around too much? Don't get upset. Roll with it; join in the fun. It's a sign that they're enjoying devotions—and that's good news!

6. *Hang in there!* I mean it. Family devotions can be tough. But remember, sometimes you have to do something you don't like to protect something you love. You love your kids and you need to protect them by helping them prepare for the battles of life. One way you do this is by teaching them in family devotional time.

As time goes on, you'll find that family devoes aren't so hard after all. You'll find the kids will really enjoy them, even look forward to them. The best thing is that you'll be helping them prepare for life in some areas that are really important. You'll never regret the effort you make to have family devotions.

I'm encouraging you to do something good for your kids—and for yourself as well. And you'll probably shock the person who gave you this book while you're at it!

C'mon. Give this book a try. You can do it!

Smashed Tomatoes

What's the Point?

Here's a messy way to teach that God can make something good out of our lives, even if we think it's hopeless.

Things You'll Need

- Big, ripe tomatoes—at least a couple for each child.
- A large, clear plastic bag to put them in when you're done.
- A hose or a bucket of water to clean up the sidewalk.

Here We Go

Grab the tomatoes, get the kids together and say something like this:

For devoes tonight we're going to go outside. I need your help with these tomatoes. We're going to *plant* them.

Expect some strange looks after this statement. Since when are *you* into gardening? It may not even be the season for planting. That's OK. You can explain a little more.

We're going to plant them on the street (or sidewalk or driveway. Don't worry—they'll have to clean it up!). Yeah, we're going to heave these in the air as high as we can and see how they look when they hit the ground.

Once outside, you'd better demonstrate. This probably breaks some carefully cultivated family rules; normally you wouldn't allow the kids to go smashing tomatoes (at least, I hope not!). That's exactly what makes this fun for the kids. If they're having fun, they'll learn and remember better. Toss that tomato as high as you can. Try not to hit the kids. Then get them involved.

OK, kids—now it's your turn. Each of you take a tomato, and one at a time you're going to throw it as high in the air as you can.

Let them have fun here. If a tomato lands and it isn't pulverized, you may ask them to step on it a couple of times or throw it again. When all the smashing is done, you'll have to get them to clean up.

OK, kids. Let's pick up this mess. Scoop these tomatoes up and put them back in the plastic bag.

You may need to hose the area down or throw a bucket of water on it. Now, hold the bag up so everyone can see it and ask them something like this:

What should we do with this bag of smashed tomatoes? Should we put it back in the fridge?

They'll probably think you ought to throw the tomatoes out. Perfect. Now it's time to bring some meaning to this little tomato tantrum.

Remember Moses in the Bible? His countrymen were slaves to the Egyptians, yet Moses lived in the ruling Pharaoh's household. He was growing into a position where he might really be able to help his people. His concern for how badly his people were being treated grew until one day he made a terrible mistake. He saw an Egyptian man hurting one of the slaves. Moses rushed over to help the slave. Instead of just stopping the Egyptian, Moses killed him. He blew it! Now he was a criminal, a fugitive. He had to leave Pharaoh's house and escape into the desert. He was like one of these smashed tomatoes—useless and hopeless. All his big plans of helping his people went into the garbage.

Now to really sew this up right, end your devoes with a dinner made from tomatoes, such as spaghetti, lasagna or ravioli—but don't expect to use the tomatoes you started off with!

Of course, the story doesn't end there. God had His own plan. He continued to train Moses out in the desert. Moses didn't know it then, but someday God would make him one of the greatest leaders of all time. He would return to Egypt to do more than just *help* his people. He would set them *free*.

Tie It Together

This bag of smashed tomatoes may not look very good or useful to you, but it is. We're going to have spaghetti *(or lasagna or ravioli, etc.)* tonight. If you don't smash tomatoes, you won't have any sauce. That wouldn't be so great. You put smashed tomatoes into the hands of a chef and you get things like spaghetti, lasagna, ravioli, taco sauce, ketchup, salsa and tomato soup.

Instead of rattling off all these yourself, you may want to give them one or two and then get their input. See how many foods they can name that have smashed tomatoes in them.

Now, we're not really going to use *these* tomatoes—they're all dirty now. But the fact is, a smashed tomato can really be useful in the hands of a chef.

God is like a chef. He can make really good things out of what we might call a mess. Sometimes people do something wrong and they only see the mistake they made or the mess they're in. That's happened to me (*can you give an example?*) and it will happen to you. Some people turn to drugs, alcohol, suicide or plenty of other things because they can't stand the mess they've made of their life.

We need to turn to God. Just like a chef can make great things from smashed tomatoes, God can make great things from your life when you give it totally to Him. Remember Moses?

Sometimes you just don't feel like God can use you. It may not be because you've blown it in some big way. Maybe you just don't feel good enough or special enough. When you look in a mirror you don't see much that God can use. You're like a smashed tomato. Well, the good news is that God can do some pretty amazing things through you.

The Bible demonstrated that fact with the story of the boy who gave his lunch to Jesus. It wasn't much to offer. Just five loaves and two fishes. But what did Jesus do? He multiplied the food and fed thousands of hungry people with it.

Maybe you've really blown it. Maybe you just don't see much potential in yourself. Maybe you wish you were more athletic, more good-looking or more popular with other kids. Never give up on yourself. Give yourself to God and watch what He can do.

References

Exodus chapters 2-14; John 6:1-14

Bottle Rockets & the Meaning of Life

What's the Point?

Shoot a rocket up into space, and show your kids why they were put down here on earth.

Things You'll Need

- Matches
- A glass bottle
- Several small bottle rockets
- A nice clear area to launch the rockets
- A garden hose or a bucket of water

Keep It Legal!

Make sure bottle rockets and other fireworks are permitted in your area before embarking on this devotional adventure. Also, resist the urge to buy the big, powerful ones; the standard model will do just fine.

Here We Go

OK, OK, "the meaning of life" may seem like a ridiculously tough topic to tackle for family devoes. But it's a pretty important topic, and we can't afford to avoid it. Think about all the problems kids—and adults—set themselves up for because they've lost touch with why they exist in the first place. Before they know it, they start acting like life is all about making themselves happy. A lot of people spend the majority of their life trying to do just that. Come to think of it, sometimes I do too—a lot more often than I care to admit. Same with you? I kind of thought so.

Well, then, if we're going to teach a spiritual lesson as big as "the meaning of life," we'll have to keep it simple—simple enough so that maybe you and I can learn something, too.

Bring the bottle rocket gear to your launch site. It would be ideal to do this when the sky is getting a little dark so you can see the spark trail the rockets leave behind. You might say something like this:

Tonight I brought some bottle rockets. Anybody want to help me launch 'em?

I expect you'll have some very willing volunteers. Great! Just be sure you've gone over the basic safety rules first, OK?

1. Make a circle in the dirt around the bottle with a radius of at least fifteen feet. Everyone has to stand outside the circle as soon as the fuse is lit. (Make sure the rest of your rockets are outside the circle too!)

2. Have that bucket of water or garden hose handy. If a rocket seems to be a dud, douse it with water before you touch it.

Let them shoot off all the rockets. They'll love it, and it will help engrave the lesson in their heads. Shooting off a couple of dozen bottle rockets will also increase the chances of getting a "dud" or one that flies crazily off-course. A rocket like that can help illustrate a point you'll want to make later in the lesson.

When the flyin' is done, say something like this:

Do you have any idea why bottle rockets like the ones we've been shooting are made in the first place?

Get their opinions here. There really isn't a "right" answer, but here's what you're looking for:

Bottle rockets are made for the enjoyment of the one who owns them. They make these sparkling sweethearts so someone like you or me can get a kick out of watching them sail into the sky.

If the kids didn't quite give the answer you were looking for, help them out. Then take it a little farther to make sure they're tracking with you.

Does that make sense to you? I mean, if it wasn't any fun to watch bottle rockets fly, nobody would buy them. If nobody bought them, the bottle rocket makers of this world would be out of a job. So bottle rockets are made for the pure enjoyment of the one flying them.

What do you like *best* about flying bottle rockets?

Anything goes here. If you get no response, tell them what *you* like best. Is it the anticipation as you light the fuse? The trail of sparks as it flies through the air? The popping sound it makes at the end of the flight?

How do you feel about a "dud"?

If you had a dud or two you can use as an example, great. If not, they'll have to use their imagination. Anyway, they probably don't get all that excited about a dud. A dud is a disappointment.

I hate duds. I feel cheated when I light a bottle rocket and it turns out to be a dud. I've been thinking that in some ways, *we* can be like bottle rockets. God has designed us for *His* use, *His* enjoyment. When we live the way He designed us to live, He gets great enjoyment out of it.

God gave us life in the first place. He made us. When we gave Him control of our life, when we became Christians, it was like He lit our fuse. We took off, leaving a trail of things behind us, things we do for Him: telling our friends about Him; praying to Him; desiring to be close to Him. These are like sparks coming out of the bottle rocket.

Let me read you some verses from the Bible.

> For we are God's workmanship, created in Christ Jesus to do good works, which God prepared in advance for us to do.
>
> (Ephesians 2:10)

> For he chose us in him before the creation of the world to be holy and blameless in his sight. In love he predestined us to be adopted as his sons through Jesus Christ, in accordance with his pleasure and will.
>
> (1:4-5)

> Finally, brothers, we instructed you how to live in order to please God, as in fact you are living. Now we ask you and urge you in the Lord Jesus to do this more and more.
>
> (1 Thessalonians 4:1)

> So we make it our goal to please him.
>
> (2 Corinthians 5:9)

Tie It Together

Just like a bottle rocket is made for our enjoyment, *we* are made for *God's* enjoyment. What do you think about that?

See what they say here. I had you talking a little long just now. Hey, we want to teach them a little morsel of truth, not stuff them until they're sick.

If we're made for God's enjoyment, what about all the things we do for our *own* enjoyment?

Great question. How do you answer this one? Try saying something like this after you've given them a chance to mull it over for themselves:

In our culture this is a real problem. People forget God made them for *His* enjoyment. They spend their life trying to make themselves happy, which can lead to trouble. If their life *doesn't* bring God enjoyment, it amounts to a "dud" in God's eyes.

What should *we* do? Remember why we exist in the first place. If you have it clear in your mind that you exist to please God, it affects how you live. It will change how you make decisions. You won't merely ask, "What will make *me* happy?" but "What will make *God* happy?"

Are the kids still with you? Make your point, but don't overdo it (I tend to try too hard to drive the point home). There is a lot more we could say, but it's probably time to wrap it up.

I can't stand bottle rockets that are "duds" or that go off on some crazy direction of their own instead of where I aim them. We don't want to be "duds" to God. We don't want to go off in our own direction. Let's remember we exist to bring *Him* enjoyment. If we do that, we'll have a life with meaning and purpose. And the truth of it is, when we try to make *Him* happy, we'll find it makes *us* happy too!

Nobody Will Know

What's the Point?

You're going to pull off the "perfect" prank as you illustrate that God sees everything we do—even if no one else does.

Things You'll Need

- A secret accomplice with a video camera
- A package of toilet paper
- A fast car for a quick getaway (Just kidding!)

Here We Go

Here's the plan: You're going to "toilet paper" the house of a friend, relative or neighbor. Try to pick someone fairly close to home, and someone who won't press charges in the event the police happen to catch you in the process of "decorating." (You probably want to do this when there is no rain predicted, since cleaning up soggy toilet paper is a real drag.)

Next, you'll need to have an accomplice who will be hiding somewhere near the house you're hitting. Your accomplice will use the video camera to tape the whole event from the moment you and the kids arrive. Your friend with the video should cover the little red indicator light on the front of the camera with a piece of black electrical tape, and find a good hiding spot where he can record the action but won't be spotted by the kids. Keep that in mind when you're selecting your target. In fact, a great way to do this is to have your intended "victim" be your accomplice, who could do the videotaping from inside his own house. (That should end any fears you may have about getting arrested!)

Tell your accomplice to get some close-up "zoom" shots so you'll be able to recognize each person involved in the raid. If you do this in the evening, try to select a home that has a street light nearby. That should give you enough light to do the job.

You might start out saying something like this:

OK, guys. It's time for family devotions. We're going to visit (*fill in the targeted person's name here*). We're going to bring along some toilet paper. A whole lot of toilet paper, in fact. *(Bring out the package of toilet paper.)*

When I was in high school, we'd "TP" someone's house to show them how much we appreciated them. I think *(person's name)* would like to feel appreciated, don't you?

At this point they should be enjoying the thought of this friendly raid. Keep excitement high as you drive to the house by reviewing good "TP" strategy. Talk over where you're going to start the job and remind them to be very quiet. You don't want to get caught!

When you get there, try to keep the group in prime view of the hidden camera as much as possible. When the job is done, make a hasty escape, then stop someplace for a quick treat before you go home. While you're snacking, you can talk and laugh about the "perfect" prank and the fact that you didn't get caught. Unless one of you talks, nobody will ever know who did the deed. That's a good feeling, so you might as well enjoy it with them for all it's worth.

Your accomplice has been busy in the meantime. He's put the videotape in a plastic bag and hung it on your front door before you get home. It needs to be in a pretty obvious spot. The accomplice needs to put a note inside that might say something like this: "I think you will find this tape to be very *interesting.*"

When you pull up to the house, someone is bound to see the bag. If they don't, point to it and say, "What's that?" After they read the note, suggest that you all go in and view the tape immediately.

As they see themselves on the tape, "caught in the act," they'll probably be trying to figure out who taped it and how they knew. Now it's time for a little Scripture.

Guys, it looks like we've been caught. Let me read a couple of verses to you.

> For a man's ways are in full view of the
>   LORD,
>   and he examines all his paths.

>   (Proverbs 5:21)

Now listen to this statement that is repeated three times in Matthew, chapter 6:

> Your [Heavenly] Father . . . sees what is done in secret.

>   (Matthew 6:4, 6 and 18)

Tie It Together

Well, it looked like we had the perfect prank going there. We did a great "TP" job and it looked like we got away with it. How could we have known that we were being taped the whole time?

The verses I just read remind us that God always sees and always knows what we do. It's like He has a videotape rolling on us all the time. The truth is, we can *never* do *anything* that nobody will ever know about. God always sees; He always knows.

If you had known someone had a video camera on you when we went to "TP" the house, would you still have done it?

Who knows what kind of answer you'll get here. If they say, "No," that's great. If they're older, they may say, "Yeah, I'd do it anyway." Whatever answer they give is OK. You're still getting your point across, even if they don't want to admit it.

We do a lot of things in life when nobody is watching that we might not do if someone were. We certainly wouldn't do it if we knew it was being recorded by a hidden camera.

If you find yourself checking to see if anybody is looking before you do something, remember *God is*. He sees everything; we never really "get away" with anything.

You don't have to go on and on about this—you've gotten your point across. A more sensitive kid may be feeling a bit guilty at this point—whether about the "TP" job or something else—so you need to address the forgiveness issue. Just ask them what they think you should do with the tape. They'll probably advise you to erase it. That opens the door to remind them that if we ask forgiveness, God is faithful to "erase the tape" on us, too.

Y'know, there's something else that follows forgiveness—it's called *restitution*.

That means making something right when we've done something wrong. If we've stolen something, we give it back; if we've lied about something, we need to set the record straight. And for us, it means going back and cleaning up the mess we've made. Let's go!

Target Practice

What's the Point?

Use a BB gun to show how we need to aim carefully if we want to hit the targets God has for us in life.

Things You'll Need

- A BB gun (about $20 at most department stores, or borrow one)
- Three or four plastic milk cartons filled with water for targets
- A protective back-board

The milk cartons make great targets. A BB will go right through the plastic, leaving a stream of water shooting out to prove the target was hit. For the protective backboard, use something like a piece of plywood, an old mattress or the side of a shed.

Here We Go

This is one of those devoes that is best done outdoors—for obvious reasons. It may seem long, but it's pretty fast-paced. Besides, the BB gun will help hold their attention. Keep the gun hidden until you're ready to start. You might tell them something like this:

I've got something here you're gonna enjoy.

Pull out the BB gun. Let them "oooh" and "ahhh" over it for a moment.

We're going to go outside for a little target practice.

Go outside, set up your target(s), make sure they know how to handle the BB gun safely and let them shoot. Move the target close enough so they hit it. After everyone has hit the target once or twice, take the gun and talk a little more.

You did really well! You hit the target! All right, tell me how you did it.

Get their input. They'll probably say that they aimed. Ask them to explain how you "aim." You're looking for them to say something like, "You keep one eye on the target and point the gun in the same direction." Help them find the right words to explain it if necessary, then move on.

OK, I can see you know how to hit the target when you're looking at it. Let's see how well you do when you're not.

You can blindfold them or just have them look off to the side when they shoot. Don't let them visually aim at the target. Be careful here—we don't want any broken windows! Anyway, they should do miserably. So far so good. You've got 'em right where you want 'em.

Well, you didn't do so good this time. In fact, that was horrible shooting! You didn't even come close to the target. How come?

They should say it was because you didn't let them aim.

Aiming is really important. If you don't keep your eye on the target and point your gun at it, you're gonna miss. Y'know, God has some "targets" He wants *us* to hit too. I'm not talking about milk cartons. I'm talking about things God wants us to *become* as Christians. Becoming what God wants takes careful aiming, just like hitting a target with a BB gun. Let's look at a few verses.

There are a lot of verses here; you may want to pick and choose. Remember not to overload your kids with too much information at this point.

> How can a young man keep his
>   way pure?
> By living according to [God's] word.
> I seek you with all my heart;
>   do not let me stray from your
>   commands.
> I have hidden your word in my heart
>   that I might not sin against you. . . .

If Great Aunt Matilda is visiting . . .

If you're not comfortable with your kids using a BB gun, you could "water it down" a little by using a squirt gun (pun intended!). If you use a squirt gun, you might use candles for targets.

I meditate on your precepts
and consider your ways.
I delight in your decrees;
I will not neglect your word.

(Psalm 119:9-11, 15-16)

Therefore, holy brothers, who share in the heavenly calling, fix your thoughts on Jesus. . . . Let us fix our eyes on Jesus, the author and perfecter of our faith.

(Hebrews 3:1, 12:2)

So we fix our eyes not on what is seen, but on what is unseen. For what is seen is temporary, but what is unseen is eternal.

(2 Corinthians 4:18)

Tie It Together

God has a definite target He'd like all of us to hit. He wants us to be more and more like Jesus. Unless we aim at that, we'll never hit it. We have to "fix our eyes" on Jesus. How can we do that?

Get them thinking here. They'll have to be in the Word to keep their eyes on Him. They can't get distracted, looking this way or that way.

What happens to my aim if I don't hold the gun steady? How do I keep myself steady as I "aim" to be more like Jesus?

See what they say here. You can talk about consistency—regular personal devotions and a regular review of their life. Did I act more or less like Jesus today than I did yesterday? How was my attitude today? Most importantly, encourage them to pray for God to help them grow to be more like Jesus.

That verse I read from Psalm 119 asks this question: "How can a young man keep his way pure?" It's asking, "How do you keep on target? How do you stay on course as a Christian?" It gives the answer there in the rest of the verse: "By living according to [God's] word."

If you want to hit God's target, if you want to be more like Jesus, you'll need to be in the Word. Not just reading, but *heeding* (that means doing what it says). You have to work at it—all the time. Psalm 119 goes on to tell us how we need to *want* to hit God's target, *pray* for His help, *memorize* so we don't forget and *keep it in mind* as we go through the day (119:10-11 and 15). Verse 16 talks about how important it is to read the Bible daily and how it should be something you enjoy.

Well, there are a lot more verses I could share about the targets God wants us to hit and how we can do it. It's a lot like shooting a BB gun. You have to practice if you want to do it well. I hope that you'll want to be a sharpshooter for God—taking careful aim, fixing your eyes on Jesus and hitting the targets He has for you.

Here's one last thing for you to think about: Have your ever heard of Rehoboam

[*Ray-ha-BOW-um*]? He was the son of King Solomon. He had a lot of potential, and could have been a great king, but he blew it! You know why? Here's what the Bible says:

He did evil because he had not set his heart on seeking the LORD. (2 Chronicles 12:14)

Remember when I wouldn't let you see the target when you shot the BB gun? You didn't hit the target that way. It's the same with God's targets for your life. If you don't take careful aim like we talked about you'll do worse than just miss. You'll do wrong—evil. Guaranteed. It's our nature.

See why this is so important?

You can end in prayer here, or, if you still have their attention, talk about some people you admire who hit the target or are growing more like Christ. You might even talk about some who could have, but didn't. You can think of plenty of Bible examples. Help them build an appetite for being "on target" Christians.

Have a little more "fun" time at the end; let them shoot the gun again. It's another way to help them remember the lesson you're trying to teach. When you're done, empty out the BBs and keep the gun somewhere visible. Better yet, give it to one of the kids. Talk about a great reminder!

Odometer Odyssey

What's the Point?

This will help you "drive" home the point that, just like a car, your Christian life needs regular maintenance if you expect it to last for the long haul.

Things You'll Need

- A car with a lot of miles on it—the more miles the better. No kidding, that's all you need.

Here We Go

Take the family for a little drive. It would be great to do this when your odometer is ready to turn over to a nice fat number like 100,000 miles. Drive just far enough to get the odometer to turn over to the number you want them to see. If it's possible, try to get the kids to watch it actually turn. Next, pull into the parking lot of a fast-food restaurant or ice cream shop. It's time to teach.

Well, you've just seen the car turn over to (*you fill in the amount*) miles. That's not something you see every day. In fact, in my whole life I've only seen a car turn this many miles maybe (*you fill in the amount*) other time(s).

Here's a couple of fun facts you may be able to use to give the kids a perspective of how many miles are on your odometer. Earth is almost 25,000 miles around at the equator. If you have 100,000 miles logged on your car, it's like going around the world four times! The moon sits about 240,000 miles from the earth. If you have 120,000 miles on the car, it's like driving halfway to the moon!

When this car was brand new it was in perfect condition. It had a lot of company, too. There were hundreds of cars in the lot with it. I don't know where all those other cars are today, but it's a pretty safe bet that some aren't even running anymore. Some probably got wrecked in accidents; others were probably not taken care of, so they aren't dependable anymore.

If you want your car to last for as many miles as this one, what types of things do you need to do?

Get their input . . . oil and filter changes, tune-ups, tires and other regular maintenance. Sometimes a mechanic needs to make adjustments to bring the car back to proper "specs."

With the right maintenance, a car can last a long time. Like I said, it's not very often you'll see a car turn this many miles. I'll tell you something else you don't see very often: people that really go the distance for Christ; people that are good, dependable Christians over the long haul; people who remain solid Christians for a lifetime.

You'll find that to be the case with your friends. Only a few will be strong, committed Christians for their entire life. Some go "off roading" somewhere during their teen years. Some never get back on the road to a life that counts for Christ. Others get wrecked. They forget that the devil wants to mess them up. They let down their guard and *wham!* The devil wins. Some get careless, and their car gets stolen—they lose their faith.

Let me read a couple of verses to you:

Enter through the narrow gate. For wide is the gate and broad is the road that leads to destruction, and many enter through it. But small is the gate and narrow the road that leads to life, and only a few find it.

(Matthew 7:13-14)

Be self-controlled and alert. Your enemy the devil prowls around like a roaring lion looking for someone to devour. Resist him, standing firm in the faith.

(1 Peter 5:8-9)

And let us run with perseverance the race marked out for us.

(Hebrews 12:1)

Tie It Together

If I want my car to last for a long time, I've got to be sure I have the proper maintenance done, like oil changes. A car can be a great tool. It can give you the ability to do things you'd never dream of doing without one. If you neglect the maintenance, you're liable to end up on foot.

Too many times I've seen kids neglect the "maintenance" of their faith. What type of things am I talking about here?

Get their input. Reading the Bible, praying and growing in Christ.

These kids end up in wrecks. They wreck their life with poor choices and by doing things they never should have done as a Christian.

They may have started out strong when they were young, but they don't keep up with the maintenance and they end up in the junkyard.

My hope for you is that you grow stronger and stronger as a Christian. I want you to finish the race of life well. The key is being consistent. Just like oil changes on a car. Can you imagine someone putting 50,000 miles on their car without an oil change? They're in trouble. Can you imagine them trying to make up for it by giving the car a bunch of frantic oil changes right in a row? That's crazy. Everybody knows that won't work. The damage is done by that time.

The sad thing is, a lot of kids live their life like that. They neglect the Bible and the basic spiritual maintenance needed for their life. The devil and his demons are looking for kids like that. They want to "devour" them. That doesn't sound good to me.

Then when trouble comes, these kids think they can just dust off their Bible and fix everything quick. All too often, the damage is done. There is no quick fix. If they had only been consistent with their Christian life, they wouldn't have had the trouble in the first place.

Consider this: How are *you* going to live? Are you going to keep up with the "maintenance" and go the distance, or are you going to coast along and take things as they come? I pray that you keep up with the maintenance.

Whoa, I got a little "preachy" here. You'll have to adjust the intensity of your words to what you feel your kids can handle. It's a pretty intense subject, though—the stakes are high.

There's a simple way to lighten this up a bit, though. Since you're in the parking lot of a fast-food restaurant or ice cream place, tell the kids you're all going in for ice cream or a snack to celebrate the number of miles on your car. Remind them that a life lived for Christ will be rewarded someday too.

This Little Light of Mine

What's the Point?

We're to be like Christ. Sound like too tall an order? Your kids will discover that in a dark world, even the smallest of lights makes a difference.

Things You'll Need

- A gas, oil or electric camping lantern, or (as a last resort) a large flashlight
- Miniature key chain versions of the same thing—one for each kid

You can usually find lanterns, with matching keychains that light up, in a hardware or camping store. The important thing is to have them look similar, but one should be much bigger and more powerful than the others.

Here We Go

Find a good, dark place for this devotional activity—preferably outdoors, because I'm not so sure you want to fire up a lantern in the house. (This one is great for a camping trip.) Keep the small lanterns or flashlights out of sight for now. You might start out with something like this:

I'm holding one of the key items to pack when you go camping: a lantern. Campers depend on a lantern like this to help them set up their campsite, to cook by and to find their way around in the dark. Sometimes campers turn up a lantern to full power and set it by their tent while they're out getting firewood so they can find their way back to camp. The darker it is, the more you'll appreciate a good lantern. It would be downright scary without it.

You know, this lantern reminds me of Jesus in some ways. Give me some ideas of what I might mean by that.

Give them a chance to make some guesses. They'll probably come up with some of the very points you'll hit tonight. If you want to go a little deeper, ask them to tell you what they mean when they offer some ideas. They'll be teaching the lesson themselves. It's the best way to learn.

Just like this lantern, Jesus can make life a lot easier for us when we stay close to Him. We see things better when Jesus is around.

When we're not sure what to do or where to go, He helps "light" the way. Anybody have an example they could share that would show how this really works?

This question is a shot in the dark. If someone does give you an example, try not to look shocked. Just nod your head and smile. Now let's hit them with some verses.

There are tons of verses in the Bible to illustrate this, and here are a couple of them.

> When Jesus spoke again to the people, he said, "I am the light of the world. Whoever follows me will never walk in darkness, but will have the light of life."
>
> (John 8:12)

> Your word is a lamp to my feet and a light for my path.
>
> (Psalm 119:105)

Jesus is our Guide. How do we stay in His light?

The typical answer you'll get will be to stay in the Bible and do what it says. That's good, but don't beat it to death; just move on. There's still some ground to cover.

Yeah, that verse in Psalm 119 tells us that a good way to stay in His light is to stay in the Word. Basically, we need to know what the Bible says and then do it. Now if you're a Christian, the Bible says *you* are a light too. Matthew 5:14 says, "You are the light of the world." Wait a minute—I thought *Jesus* was the light. How can *I* be a light?

Get a little input from them. Try to build on whatever they say. Here's an idea of how you may continue.

We can be an example to friends for starters. God wants us to help show others the way to Him. It starts by living like a good Christian. Some kids may make fun of that, but deep down many of them may wish they had what you have.

Do you have a personal example? This would be a good time to share it. Then you'll want to pull out the miniature lantern. Turn it on and show the kids. Turn off the big lantern.

I have a miniature lantern here. It doesn't shine anywhere near as bright as the big one, but you'd be surprised at just how much good it can do when you're in a really dark spot.

Tie It Together

When we read the Bible, we see life more clearly. It shows us how we should live. It shows us what we should do and the type of person we should be. It encourages us and helps us make the right decisions. It helps to keep us from being afraid. In other words, it shows us the way. Learning what God wants us to do and then actually doing it are all part of "living in the light."

This is what your friends need to see—the right way to live. You may not think you can do much, but that's where you're underestimating the effect of even a little light.

It would be really good to get to a super dark place and only have the little light on for a while—just long enough for their eyes to adjust to the low light. You might even have someone take the light a little distance away and turn it on and off. As dim as it may seem, you can still see it. When you're ready, let's wrap it up.

Even though the light is small, it really *does* make a difference. Imagine we had someone stand with this light really far away. Imagine we had to find our way to that person in total darkness. What would happen if that person turned off his light as you were trying to find your way to him?

Get their input or just move on, whatever you think.

Every time you stop living like a Christian, it's like turning off your light. It's really easy to do that. Complaining, arguing, having a bad attitude or plenty of other things you could come up with would be enough to douse the effect of your light.

I have one of these little lights for each of you tonight. When you see it, remember that we're to be a light, just like Jesus. We aren't as bright, but we can still do a lot of good in a dark world.

A fun way to end this might be to turn off all the lights for a moment, then have each person turn on his light, one at a time.

Parable of the Stock Car Race

What's the Point?

Have a fun time with your kids—and also get them thinking about accomplishing something in life, rather than just going around in circles.

Here We Go

After you have your tickets or the date and time of the stock car race, let the family in on your plans ahead of time. When they hear that you'll be going to a stock car race as part of your family devoes, they'll really be anticipating the event. When the big day arrives, go and enjoy the stock car races. Save the teaching for later.

After the race is over, try to go out for some ice cream. They'll remember the event even more if you do. (Besides, as I'm writing this I have a taste for ice cream. I have to work it into this lesson somehow!) Anyway, wipe the hot fudge from your chin and say something like this:

Well, how was a *stock car race* for openers to devotions this week? We're going to learn something from God's Word tonight with a little help from the stock car races we saw.

Tell me about some of your favorite parts of the races.

Give them some time to think and to throw in their thoughts. They may talk about a car crash, a near miss, a close finish or maybe a little bumping action on the track. Whatever it is, great. You might even tell them some of the highlights for you. When the time is right, move on.

I wonder how far they drive in these races. I mean, how many miles is an average race? Got any ideas?

Let them guess here. Get them to throw out a number.

40

The funny thing is that with all that hard driving, bumping and speed, they really didn't *go* anywhere. Y'know what I mean? They ended the race in about the same spot they started. They were going in circles. Those drivers were probably going ninety miles per hour out there, but they weren't *getting* anywhere!

That's exactly how some kids are going through life. They're speeding along, but they're just going in circles. They aren't *going* anywhere. Sure, they're busy. They have a lot of activities. They're looking for a good opportunity or a chance to get ahead somehow. The thing is, they don't really get anywhere that counts in the long run. It can happen easily—to adults as well as kids.

You know, life is like a race. It can be exciting, dangerous, fun and even hard at times. The key is, we're supposed to *get* somewhere. God doesn't want us going around in circles. He wants us to accomplish some things in life. Things *He* has planned for us.

Let me read you a few verses.

> Your word is a lamp to my feet
>   and a light for my path.

> (Psalm 119:105)

> Trust in the LORD with all your heart
>   and lean not on your own
>   understanding;
> in all your ways acknowledge him,
>   and he will make your paths straight.

> (Proverbs 3:5-6)

On a Budget?

If the local racetrack is too pricey or too far away, pick up a video at the library or a rental store about stock car or any other car racing. You can still get the point across—it just may not stick in their memory like it will if they actually go to a race.

You have made known to me the path of
>   life;
> you will fill me with joy in your presence,
> with eternal pleasures at your right
>   hand.

(Psalm 16:11)

Tie It Together

There's a ton of good stuff in those verses, but we're only going to hit a couple quick points. God has a plan for each of you. It may be exciting sometimes and boring other times. It may be fun, or it may be not so fun. Sometimes it's going to hurt, and nobody on earth will be able to make you feel better.

And because the devil is real, he's always interested in finding a way to mess you up and make you crash. He'll destroy you if he can. I guess that makes being a Christian dangerous too.

God's way, His plan for your life, is the only way to go. It's the one that leads to eternal satisfaction. In other words, if you take God's path you'll never regret it. You'll be very happy you did it His way.

How do I know what I'm supposed to do? Any ideas?

Let's see where they're at. Are they tracking with you? Give them a moment to speak, then try to work with what they give you. You may end up saying something like this:

The Bible tells about *how* we're to live—what kind of people God wants us to become, how we're to love others and so on. Then we ask God to direct us as we face choices and decisions. We ask Him to make the path straight—you know, clear or obvious. That definitely implies giving God control of our life too.

If we do that, God will direct our path through life so that we find true contentment and lasting pleasure. It sounds good, but it isn't easy. We have to keep working at it, but it's worth it.

How are you doing? Are you just racing with the pack? Tell God tonight that you don't want to just go in circles, that you want to take His path and accomplish all He has planned for you.

If you think they're making that kind of commitment, you may want to talk further with them, laying out some specifics as to where to start.

Human Dartboard

What's the Point?

Here's a graphic way to encourage your kids to show love to their siblings, instead of taking "shots" at them.

Things You'll Need

- A picture of each kid that will be in the devotional session—the bigger the photo, the better.
- Several darts
- A dartboard or some kind of backboard

The photo(s) can be a group shot of everyone or separate photos of each person. Don't use any pictures you are very attached to, because unless everyone is a really bad aim, the photos will be destroyed by the time you're done. You can probably borrow the darts and dartboard if you don't have your own set. Ask around— someone probably has one in the garage somewhere. Anyway, if you decide to buy one, don't get anything fancy.

Here We Go

This activity can be done indoors, but it's a little safer taking it outside, unless you really enjoy patching walls. Find a good spot to hang your dartboard and get the kids together. You might start out this way:

OK, gang. For devoes tonight we're going to play darts. Lets go outside and have a little fun.

I'd suggest going over a few safety rules before handing them any darts. Keep the rules simple, because you can't expect them to listen too carefully. They'll just want to get their hands on those darts.

After a quick demonstration of the right way to throw darts (which is really just an excuse to get the first turn), you might have each of them get a number of throws at the dartboard. Now collect the darts and get their attention. Hold up one of the photos and tack it up on the dartboard. Ask them something like this:

Now who would like to throw with this picture as a target?

Expect everyone to be eager, except the one in the photo. If you're doing this with just one child, get a picture of a friend or relative. Maybe the kids will want to assign points—say, ten points in the face, twenty in the nose, etc. Now, don't get offended at this—you're going to tie this all together and illustrate an important point. The kids will love it, and that makes it easier for them to absorb what you'll teach them with this barbaric game. If you have more than one picture, routinely rotate them onto the target.

Let them have their fun. Listen to how happy they are when they land a shot right in the face of their sister, brother, cousin or whoever. That's exactly what you want.

After every picture has been thoroughly punctured, it's time to move on and bring out the application.

Well, this has been fun. Would you like to do this again sometime?

I expect your kids will be as enthusiastic about the idea as mine were. Sure, they'd like to do it again. The fact is, they've been doing it for a long time. You're about to show them what you mean. There are quite a few verses here. It's a progression of thought. First the Bible says we should love our brothers, then we give some examples of what real love is. The verses in First John 2 are referring to Christian "brothers," but it works for siblings as well.

Let me read some verses to you.

Anyone who claims to be in the light but hates his brother is still in the darkness. Whoever loves his brother lives in the light, and there is nothing in him to make him stumble. But whoever hates his brother is in the darkness and walks around in the darkness; he does not know where he is going, because the darkness has blinded him.

(1 John 2:9-11)

This is the message you heard from the beginning: We should love one another. Do not be like Cain, who belonged to the evil one and murdered his brother.

(3:11-12)

You have heard that it was said to the people long ago, "Do not murder, and anyone who murders will be subject to judgment." But I tell you that anyone who is angry with his brother will be subject to judgment.

(Matthew 5:21-22)

Love is patient, love is kind. It does not envy, it does not boast, it is not proud. It is not rude, it is not self-seeking, it is not easily angered, it keeps no record of wrongs. Love does not delight in evil but rejoices with the truth. It always protects, always trusts, always hopes, always perseveres. Love never fails.

(1 Corinthians 13:4-8)

This is how we know what love is: Jesus Christ laid down his life for us. And we ought to lay down our lives for our brothers. . . . Dear children, let us not love with words or tongue but with actions and in truth.

(1 John 3:16, 18)

Tie It Together

You really seemed to enjoy throwing darts at someone else's picture. The truth of it is, that's pretty similar to what we often do in real life. Anybody know what I mean by that?

It's important to get their input. They may bring up the point you're trying to make. If they bring it up, then you end up discussing their ideas. If you have to bring it up, they may look at it as a lecture. You want to avoid a lecture if you can. In either case, you need to make the point clear.

In real life we can often take "shots" at brothers or sisters or other people close to us. We give little verbal "digs" or "jabs" at them. We know their weak points, and we know what can hurt them most. With a little practice, we get pretty good at it. Just like the dart game we played, we can get to be pretty good at hurting each other. Give me some examples of how we do that.

Listen close and you'll hear about hurts you probably didn't know existed. This wouldn't be a great time to make a joke about someone's input. If they seem stuck, you may need to give them some examples. Here's a few to get you thinking: criticizing, embarrassing them in front of others, making fun of them, laughing at them, arguing, fighting, the list goes on.

This is serious stuff. It won't be easy to get them to see the light here. We're hoping for progress. It starts with their seeing the problem and realizing it should be different.

OK, in light of the things you've just described and the verses I read a few minutes ago, what are some things you *should* be doing? How should you treat each other?

If you get enough input from them here, you won't have to add a thing. Hopefully, they'll say they should love each other more. They may say they shouldn't argue or fight, or that they should encourage each other. This is all great. Now you want to turn their good intentions into a commitment.

It's really important that we help each other and encourage each other. God wants to use each of us to help build each other up. How can we remember to do this?

See what they say here. If they have *any* idea at all, hey, that's great. If they're stumped, throw out a couple of ideas. Certainly they can pray that God will help them have compassion on others more. You may want to take those pictures you used for target practice and hang them up somewhere like the fridge as a visual reminder. Post the verses you read above them and they'll make even more of an impact. Come up with a plan as a family. You don't want to just talk about it, you want to make a difference in "actions and truth" as you read in First John 3:18.

Whatever you do, put it on the calendar to talk about it as a family every week for a while—"Hey, how are we doing with brotherly love?" When you see some unkind things going on between siblings, take them aside after things cool down and gently talk it over with them. Let them see if their actions lined up with what your devoes were all about. When you see them doing the "right" things, don't miss the chance to compliment them.

When you're done, close in prayer—and then go outside with the kids and play more darts!

Get a Grip

What's the Point?

An outing on a boat illustrates how all of us need anchors in our lives to keep us from drifting away from where we ought to be.

Things You'll Need

- A boat with an anchor
- A can of soda for each person
- A large, black plastic bag
- Ice (to keep the soda cool)
- A couple of good-sized rocks
- A long piece of rope

Put the soda, ice and rocks in the plastic bag. Tie it up with one end of the rope so the kids won't see what you have inside. Now you have a homemade anchor in addition to the anchor already inside the boat.

Here We Go

When you're out in the boat with the kids, find a good place to stop. If it is windy or there are enough waves to make you drift, that would be perfect. Cut the motor or stop rowing and say something like this:

This is the spot. This is exactly where I want to stay while we have devoes. How can I make sure I don't drift?

Sure it's a silly question, but make 'em give you the answer anyway. They should point out that you need an anchor. So far, so good.

Yeah, you're right. Without an anchor we'll drift. We've got one right here. I've connected a homemade one with one that was here in the boat.

Have one of the kids pick up the anchor while you pick up the black bag tied to it (filled with soda and ice), and heave-ho the whole thing over the side. I should warn you, when I did this with my kids, the goofy black bag had so much air in it that my "homemade" anchor actually floated on the surface. I had to poke some holes in it before it would sink. If it happens to you too, hey, you'll get a little teasing from the kids, but that's OK. They'll just remember devoes that much better. Anyway, when it hits bottom leave plenty of slack in the line and secure it to the boat.

Now, if I didn't have this anchor set, what could happen to us?

Get their input on this. Here's the type of things you're looking for: you would drift; you wouldn't be in the spot you really wanted to be after a while; you could drift into another boat or onto the shore, etc.

You're right. Drifting to shore or into another boat could cause some real damage to the boat. And if this were a river with a waterfall downstream, we could be in some real trouble. We need an anchor. It gets a grip on the bottom and keeps us from drifting into trouble.

That's a really key statement in today's devoes, folks.

Let me read you some verses from the Bible.

> Jesus said, "If you hold to my teaching, you are really my disciples. Then you will know the truth and the truth will set you free."
>
> (John 8:31-32)

> By this gospel you are saved, if you hold firmly to the word I preached to you. Otherwise, you have believed in vain.
>
> (1 Corinthians 15:2)

> So then, brothers, stand firm and hold to the teachings we passed on to you, whether by word of mouth or by letter.
>
> (2 Thessalonians 2:15)

Tips for Desert Dwellers

If you don't live near a lake or river, save this idea for a vacation. Even so, you may find that getting access to a boat is a tall order. If you can't borrow one from a friend, maybe you can rent a rowboat someplace—as long as it includes a real anchor and some rope.

Fight the good fight, holding on to faith and a good conscience. Some have rejected these and so have shipwrecked their faith.

(1 Timothy 1:18-19)

Let us hold unswervingly to the hope we profess, for he who promised is faithful.

(Hebrews 10:23)

Having an anchor is important when you're out in a boat, but it is just as essential to have "anchors" in our life too. What are some of these "anchors" we need in our life?

Get their input. There are a number of anchors, such as God, the Bible, our faith. Parents, good friends and even our character also can be anchors that keep us from drifting.

These anchors keep us from drifting away from where we really want to be. They can keep us from drifting into trouble or danger, just like the anchor does for this boat.

Tie It Together

I tied that heavy black bag as an extra anchor to the one we already had. That was like double protection. In your own life you need to throw out as many anchors as you can to keep you from trouble. Parents, good friends, your own character, and certainly God, the Bible and your faith are the kind of anchors we need to get a firm grip and keep us from drifting.

Without an anchor, a boat will naturally drift. So will people if they don't have anchors. What if that anchor we threw overboard earlier was not tied to our boat? What good would it do?

You're bringing home a key lesson here. Their answer will probably say something about the anchor not doing any good.

If the anchor isn't tied to a boat, it can't help the boat. In the same way, we have to make sure the anchors in our life are really connected to us. If our parents are an anchor for us we can't cut them off from us. If God is to be an anchor for us, then our faith must be real. It must be our own. It must be connected securely to us.

Life is full of dangers. We need anchors to keep us from naturally drifting into them. The anchors need to be attached directly to us if we want them to do any good.

You may want to ask if they have any thoughts or questions. Try to key into the fact that their faith must be real. Too many kids get in trouble because they go through adolescence trying to get by believing what their parents believe. They haven't really searched out their own faith. When they start pulling away from their parents in those teen years, their faith isn't strong enough to keep them from drifting. It's like having an anchor that isn't tied to your own boat. Anyway, depending on the level your kids are at, you may or may not try to address this aspect of it.

When you're ready, have them pull up the anchor. While they're pulling, say something like this.

There are definite advantages to having anchors. Someday we'll be rewarded for being true to our faith.

Pull open the bag and distribute the ice-cold soda.

Remember, there are definite rewards attached to having anchors in your life!

Higher Flyer

What's the Point?

Model rocketry can be used to illustrate that we can't work our way to heaven, no matter how good we are.

Things You'll Need

- A model rocket kit
- A few model rocket engines
- A rocket launcher

These items can be picked up at a local hobby shop. Be sure to get an easy-to-assemble kit, since you'll have to build it one day and fly it the next. Building the rocket with the kids is fun and raises their anticipation for the next day. (If you want to make it even more fun, get a rocket for each of them. Let them paint or customize their rocket any way they want.) A launcher gets a little pricey; maybe you can team up with another family to make the purchase. You can also build your own with a few simple materials (the hobby shop or a model-rocket magazine may have instructions). Anyway, you may find it worth the investment, because once the kids get a taste of rocketing, they'll probably want to do it again.

Here We Go

Take the kids to a park or an open field where you can fly the rocket. Be sure to follow all the safety rules, or it could be dangerous. (That's also what makes it so much fun!) Make sure there is plenty of clear field downwind from the launch site—you don't want the rocket to get caught in a tree. Set up the launch pad, insert an engine in the rocket and put it on the launcher. If you are doing this with more than one child, let one ignite the rocket while the other waits downwind to retrieve it. You might say something like this:

OK, we're ready to go. When the rocket blasts off, keep your eye on it or we'll lose it. Let's do a countdown.

Do your 10, 9, 8, 7 . . . countdown and blast that rocket away. Retrieve the rocket and do it again. It takes more time than you think. Keep going until you're out of engines or it's time to leave. Now you're ready to make your point.

Did you notice that some flights went farther than others?

Let them talk about how far their flight went. They'll probably refer to the longer flights as "better" or "good" flights. That's exactly what you want.

What if our goal was to land one of these flights on the moon? How close did we come? Do you think it would be possible for us to shoot one of these little rockets to the moon?

Let the discussion flow naturally, but of course we want them to realize they could never get one of these hobby rockets all the way to the moon if it's only powered by a little engine.

You're right. One of these rockets could never make it to the moon, unless maybe an astronaut carried it there in his *real* rocket.

That reminds me of people trying to get to heaven. Here's a Bible verse you've probably heard: "For all have sinned and fall short of the glory of God" (Romans 3:23). Notice the words "fall short." Sure, some people do good things. They don't murder, cheat or steal. But they aren't perfect. The Bible says nobody is. If they think they can get into heaven just by being good, they're in for a big shock.

People are sort of like these rockets. Some may go higher or farther than others, but not one can make it to the moon on their own. Some people may be better, or do great things, but it's never enough to get them to heaven.

Tie It Together

You may have friends who think it's possible to make it to heaven based on the things they do, but they're wrong. Maybe you can use this rocket illustration to tell your friends about Jesus. What do you think?

Don't Put It into Orbit!

When you buy engines for the rocket, don't go hog-wild. Get the less powerful ones ("A" or "B" size). The bigger engines will send the rocket higher in the air, and you'll have a better chance of losing the rocket—trust me on this one!

Get a little input here and determine where your child is. This is a good time to talk to the kids about salvation. Are you certain each of them has made this decision? If so, thank the Lord. If not, take the discussion further as a group or do it later one-on-one. No matter how good the little rocket is, it isn't going to fly to the moon any more than a person will get to heaven just by being "good."

If you're certain about their decision for Christ, this might be a good time to talk to them about friends they have who are lost. They may have friends who might think "being good" is good enough. Can you challenge your child to talk to that friend?

Depending on the direction your discussion has gone, you might wrap things up like this:

After our rocket came back to earth, what did you do?

Input time again. You're looking for them to say they went and found it.

Jesus is like that. Even after we're a Christian, we fall sometimes. We might be flying high, doing what God wants us to do, and then the next thing you know we've blown it somehow—we sinned. Well, Jesus knows where we're at. He picks us up and fixes us up so we can fly again. Ultimately, He'll take us higher than we can ever get on our own. And someday, if you've given your life to Jesus, He'll take you to heaven.

Fishing Lesson

What's the Point?

A fishing trip is an opportunity to warn your kids about the devil's schemes to "hook" us with appealing bait.

Things You'll Need

- A fishing pole
- A tackle box full of nasty-looking lures
- A nice fishing spot

It would be ideal to do this one on a camping trip. Even if fishing isn't your thing, don't skip this one! The lesson you'll teach to the kids is critical. Since we're talking about the devil in this devotional, a lure made by Eppinger called "Dardevle" (sounds like dare-devil) is a good one to have in your box. I bought a lure for each of my kids and gave it to them at the end of this lesson—I removed the hooks with a pair of wire cutters, of course! A "declawed" lure makes a nice key chain and is a good reminder of this lesson.

Here We Go

Get the kids together and grab your fishing gear. You might start out by saying something like this:

You know, you can tell someone who is really into fishing by looking at his tackle box. Let's take a look at what we have in here. Check out some of these lures.

Open the tackle box and let them look at them. Give them a little time here. If you try to get into the lesson too fast, their mind will still be thinking about the lures. Pull out different lures and hold them up. The bigger the variety, the better. Now get them thinking with a couple of questions:

Why do you suppose there are so many different kinds of lures?

See what they say here. If they need help, you may have to show them what you're driving at.

Different lures attract different kinds of fish. The type of lure you choose depends on where you're fishing too. You might use various types of lures for different conditions: deep water, shallow water, sandy bottom, weedy, etc.

I've got a question for you: How can one of these fake-looking lures really fool a fish? Anybody can see it's not the real thing, especially with these hooks. So why do fish bite on it?

62

Ah-h-h, we're getting to the heart of the matter now. If they're stumped, help them along a little.

The truth is, if the fish is hungry and you reel the lure by fast, the bait actually looks good. The fish doesn't even seem to notice the hooks. It may try a nibble, and when nothing happens, a bite. But instead of *getting* a meal, the fish *becomes* one!

By the time the fish realizes it's a trap, he's hooked. Now he becomes frantic, racing back and forth, trying desperately to get away. That's actually the fun part for many fishermen; they like the fight. If the fish can't break the line before the fisherman reels him in, he's dead.

Y'know, the devil is a fisherman too. He fishes for people, though. He has a "tackle box" full of lures and traps to catch people—and they're pretty effective! Some work for one kind of person, others work on other types. He knows what will work on you.

You're at an age now where the devil will be casting some lures by you—things that look good, but are wrong. He'll give you opportunities to "nibble" on some things that can be dangerous for your soul. You may take a nibble and find you can get away with it. You might even forget that the lures are a trap. The devil is setting you up for the kill.

Name me some things that he might use on someone your age—things that might look attractive or harmless, but are really wrong or dangerous.

Give them a minute here and listen. You'll be gaining some valuable insight about the kind of bait the devil may be using on some of your kid's peers—and maybe on your kids themselves. Don't feed them answers; you want to hear what they come up with. You'll probably hear things like drugs, alcohol, bad pictures/magazines, etc. When they've come up with as many as they can think of, start adding to the list with some of the more subtle types of "bait" the devil may use:

The devil can use all kinds of things. He can use the wrong friends, or even good friends doing the wrong things. Maybe you don't have any problems with drugs or alcohol or things like that. You see the "hooks" in those types of things and you'll never give those things a nibble. That's great—but don't think the devil is stumped! He has plenty of other lures, some of which are very harmless-looking. He can use TV, video games, sports, music, web surfing—anything to distract you and keep you busy, luring you away from spending time with God.

Listen to some verses from the Bible:

For a man's ways are in full view of the
    LORD,
    and he examines all his paths.

> The evil deeds of a wicked man ensnare
>   him;
>   the cords of his sin hold him fast.
> He will die for lack of discipline,
>   led astray by his own great folly.
>
> (Proverbs 5:21-23)

Sometimes we sin and then hold our breath, waiting to see if God is going to punish us. Scary, huh? But what these verses describe is even more frightening. Sometimes God doesn't even have to punish us—we end up punishing ourselves. Our lack of self-discipline causes us to bite on the devil's bait. We think we're getting away with it at first, but before we know it, we are held securely by the cords of our own sin. That sounds like a fish on a line to me! There's nothing scarier than to be caught on a line with the devil holding the other end.

Tie It Together:

What do fisherman do with the fish they catch?

You should hear them say things like eat them, sell them or mount them as a trophy.

The devil is no different. He'll devour you, sell you into the misery of sin or he'll wreck your life so everybody can see it. To him that's a "trophy." And though a good fisherman will throw a small fish back, the devil doesn't throw

back the people he catches. God is the only one who can free us from the devil's traps. That's why He sent His Son.

We need to be careful what we do, what we look at, where we go. The devil knows what bait will be hard for you to resist. He knows what will look good to you and he'll cast it your way. Will you resist him?

If you purchased a lure for each of them, this a good time to give it to them as a reminder of the devil's lures. Just like the "Dardevle" lure, the devil will dare you to take his bait.

The Egg Test

What's the Point?

How can we tell if our friends are growing in Christ? How can we tell if we are? Here's a test to find out.

Things You'll Need

- A dozen eggs, half of them hard-boiled
- A bucket of water or a garden hose for cleaning up

Here We Go

Grab the carton of eggs and take the kids outside. You'll need a hard surface, like a driveway or street to do this on. As you may have guessed by now, it's gonna get messy! Start by saying something like this:

I have a carton of eggs here. Some are hard-boiled so they're solid all the way through. Some are still raw inside. Now it's pretty hard to tell which are solid and which are soft when they're just sitting here. I'm going to teach you how you can tell which ones are hard-boiled. Anybody know the secret?

Let them throw out their ideas if they have any. They may want to pick a few up and give them a little shake. That's OK. Then pick up any egg and hold it in your hand.

The secret is simple. All you have to do is drop it.

At that moment, drop the egg on the hard surface.

You see? If the egg just cracks, it's hard-boiled. If it splatters instead, it isn't hard-boiled. See how easy that is? When the shell cracks, I just look to see what comes out.

You'll probably get all kind of protesting at this point. They may say there's really no secret to your method. Anybody can tell if an egg's hard-boiled or not by dropping it. Good. Just keep going.

All right, I'm going to give each of you a chance to try my method. Grab an egg. Tell me if you think it is hard-boiled or not before you drop it. Then, bombs away!

Give each of them a turn until all of the eggs have been "tested." Keep track of how accurate they are at guessing whether or not the egg is hard-boiled before they test it.

When you tried to guess if an egg was hard-boiled or not before you tested it, you weren't 100 percent accurate. *After* you used my little test it was a different story! My test allows you to accurately tell a hard-boiled egg from one that is not. I just see what comes out of the cracked shell. Are you impressed?

If the kids aren't all that impressed, that's fine—but it doesn't hurt to act disappointed! They know you're playing a game with them. They're just wondering where this is going. Soooo . . . let's show them.

OK, so my test wasn't so impressive. And you're probably wondering why we need a test to see if an egg is hard-boiled or not in the first place. The fact is, the test is pretty useless. But sometimes we do need some way of telling what is inside of something—like people, for instance, especially friends. You have some friends from school and church that claim to be Christians. How can you be sure? Use the "egg test" principle. See what comes out of them.

Let me read you some verses:

Don't Crack Up!

You don't want any hints as to which eggs are hard-boiled, so here's a foolproof way to cook them so that they don't crack: Put the eggs in a large pot of very cold water and place it on the stove on medium heat. When the water begins to boil, take the pot off the stove and let the eggs sit in the hot water for about twenty minutes. Then arrange them randomly in the carton with the raw eggs and give them plenty of time to cool in the refrigerator.

But the fruit of the Spirit is love, joy, peace, patience, kindness, goodness, faithfulness, gentleness and self-control. Against such things there is no law. Those who belong to Christ Jesus have crucified the sinful nature with its passions and desires. Since we live by the Spirit, let us keep in step with the Spirit.

(Galatians 5:22-26)

Tie It Together

Christians who are serious about their faith, Christians who really care about their relationship with Christ, will be different. Many kids—adults too, for that matter—take their Christianity a little too casually. They take it for granted; they coast along. The verses we just heard show us what should be evident in Christians who really take their faith seriously. You can tell what kind of Christian they are by what comes out of them, especially during pressure. Are they showing signs of the fruit of the Spirit?

Why is this important?

Get their feedback. Why *is* it important to have growing Christian friends around us?

If we have friends that are casual about their Christianity, it can rub off on us. If they are really committed, well, that will rub off on us, too. Listen to this verse:

Do not be misled: "Bad company corrupts good character." Come back to your senses as you ought, and stop sinning; for there are some who are ignorant of God—I say this to your shame.

(1 Corinthians 15:33-34)

The fact is, unless we're really careful, our "casual Christian" friends will affect *our* character. They will have a negative effect on who we are.

That leads us to other questions. How are *you* doing? What would the egg test reveal in you? What comes out of *you*? Are you more like Christ this year than last year? You need to ask yourself these questions. Ask God to develop more "Christlike" fruit of the Spirit in you.

The "egg test" is accurate. We just observe what comes out of the egg. Let's use that same idea on ourselves and our friends. What is coming out of you and your friends? What are you going to do about it?

If the conversation leads in this direction, you may want to discuss practical, loving ways in which your kids can influence their friends to live more Christlike lives.

A Thirst for Thrills

What's the Point?

Are your kids thrill-seekers? Show them how they can harness that energy to do great things for God!

Things You'll Need

- Tickets to an amusement park—one with a roller coaster or other thrill rides
- A camera (optional)
- A Bible

Here We Go

You're going to spend a little money on this one, so you might as well enjoy the anticipation for a while. I'd announce this to the family at least a week in advance. When they hear that they get to go to an amusement park for devotions, they'll be excited—and very curious. The anticipation alone may help engrave the lesson on their minds.

Most likely, your kids will want to hit the thrill rides, and a lot of them are set up to ride in pairs. If you have an odd number of people in your group who enjoy thrill rides, you may want to let one of the kids bring a friend. If you do, make sure that friend is in on the devoes too.

On the day of the big event, do your best to make it fun for everyone. Try to stay together as much as possible, but also give every person a chance to do what he wants. Bring enough money for snacks or have a cooler in the car with stuff the kids will like. Let them know that toward the end of the day you'll find a good spot at the park to have your devoes.

If you're not the type who likes to hit the coasters but your kids are, tell them you'll gladly wait on a bench for them to finish the ride. If your kids don't like thrill rides either, that's OK, but in that case ask them to at least take a look at those rides: watch the coasters twist and turn, listen to the riders scream. Take a look at how long the lines are and what type of people are in line. Then when you talk about thrill rides in your devotional time they can still relate. You may have some kids that like thrill rides and some that don't; you can use that too. Just be sure everyone gets to try some of the rides he likes.

When you feel it's the right time for devoes, pick up a snack for the kids and find a good spot to sit down. I'm going to take the viewpoint that your kids like the thrill rides. If they don't, talk about how a lot of people do. You might start out by saying something like this:

Tell me about some of the rides you liked best today.

Let them tell about it.

Which rides had the longest lines of people waiting to ride them?

They'll probably name some of the thrill rides.

Typically the longest lines are on the thrill rides—the roller coasters and such. Did you notice there weren't too many senior citizens waiting in line for those rides? What age group would you say was riding these rides most?

You're looking for them to say the riders were younger. Keep going.

Yeah, I'd have to say that most of the riders were younger. Any idea why?

This ought to be interesting. They may say that older people are "chicken." That's good—I wouldn't argue with them on this one.

Do you think some of the younger ones who are in line to ride are just a little bit afraid?

A Bit Hard on the Wallet?

This activity can get a little expensive, so it may not fit your budget. Besides, your kids may not be at the age where they enjoy roller coasters yet, so you may want to pass this one by. It can make a great impact, however, on kids who are in or nearing their teens.

I'm sure they'll agree that some kids are afraid, but they ride anyway.

All right, let's assume that some of the kids in line really are afraid and would rather not ride at all. Why do they do it anyway?

They'll probably say that the scared kids don't want their friends to know they're afraid. OK, we can use this point in a few minutes. Press on.

Let me ask you about the kids who *aren't* afraid. Why aren't they terrified of these rides?

This may be hard for them to put in words. If they're not afraid, they may not understand how anyone *can* be afraid. Regardless, you can work with whatever they give you. You're getting them to think.

It seems to me that kids, especially in the teen years, have a thirst for thrills. A roller coaster ride can get their blood pumping. Kids do all kinds of things for thrills. Can you name a few?

Try to get their input here. If you need to help them along, you might mention the way some kids drive after they've had their driver's license for a while—fast and careless. Or how about some of the things kids say—brash or gutsy things, for the thrill of showing off? And I doubt that the motion picture industry would make nearly the number of "thrillers" they do if it weren't for the dollars the younger audience pays to see them. When they've mentioned some things or you've helped them along here a bit, move on.

It seems that kids, especially teens, will throw caution to the wind easier than older folks. The government is well aware of this fact. That's why they recruit people for the military when they're still in their teen years. They're more likely to do risky things.

Let me read you an excerpt from the story of Jonathan in the Old Testament. The story takes place when Jonathan's father, Saul, was king. King Saul had a meager army of only about 600 men. The Philistines had been plaguing the nation of Israel. They formed raiding parties to swoop down on the land of the Israelites.

The Philistines captured every blacksmith in Israel, so that the Israelites could not make weapons to defend themselves. Their strategy worked; eventually weapons became so scarce that out of Saul's 600 men, only King Saul and his son Jonathan had a sword. If a farmer needed his tools sharpened, he had to go to the Philistines and pay through the nose for it. Defeated and defenseless, Saul's men began to defect to the Philistine army.

It was Jonathan whom God used in the end. Was Jonathan more open to taking a risk than the others? Probably. Let's read what happened:

Read First Samuel 13:16-14:23. I'd read it from a modern translation to make it as clear as possible. When you're done reading, move on to bring home an application.

Tie It Together

So God used Jonathan to initiate a battle with the Philistines. He gave Jonathan the guts to do what none of the other 600 soldiers dared. He trusted God's leading and walked into the face of danger—right into the enemy camp. Twenty men tried to stop him, and all twenty were cut down by Jonathan's sword.

God made the Philistines so confused they began to kill each other. The Israelites who had joined the Philistines turned and fought against them. King Saul and his men joined the battle along with others. In the end, a mighty victory was won.

Earlier we talked about the things kids do for thrills. Not too many things are what we'd consider to be "good" things. Kids have a God-given gutsy nature that is often being channeled into doing some pretty useless, even stupid, things.

Even the kids who are afraid to do some of these things get sucked in by their friends. They do things they know are wrong, or they do things they really don't want to do. That's just like a lot of the kids who ride the roller coasters even though they don't want to.

The story of Jonathan shows another way. Instead of getting thrills doing some not-so-great stuff, he got some pretty incredible thrills doing things for God.

God can lead you to plenty of excitement, if you let Him. Can you imagine Jonathan in Saul's camp? He's feeling restless. He wants to *do* something. What if he settled for pulling some pranks around the campfire? Sure, he may have gotten a little thrill, but it can't compare to the exhilaration he must have felt when he knew he was "on a mission from God"!

You've been doing a lot of talking, and hopefully some of it is sinking in. Time to wrap it up.

So, I guess that would be Jonathan's challenge to you. Don't settle for just *any* thrills. Satisfy your growing thirst for thrills by consulting God. Ask Him what He wants you to do. Then take action as He leads. Sound boring? Not when you look at what Jonathan did.

If you see things are ripe for more discussion, great. Otherwise you may want to hit some more rides before you go. This would be a good opportunity to bring out the camera. Take pictures of the kids in front of some of the roller coasters. The photos will serve as a good reminder of the truths they learned in today's devoes.

Baby Stuff

What's the Point?

A tricycle race will serve to emphasize that if we don't mature as Christians, we can really limit the things we'll be able to do.

Things You'll Need

- A tricycle—or better yet, more than one
- A jar of baby food

The plan is to have a tricycle race to start off your devotions, so it's best to have two or more. If you only come up with one, simply time each "contestant" with a stopwatch to come up with a winner.

The jar of baby food is a "prize" for the winner. Find something really nauseating, something that is likely to make them gag just reading the label. Something like "strained liver" would do it for me. (You might also plan on having a treat that they'll really like hidden on the side to snack on when devoes are over.)

Here We Go

I'd keep the trike and the baby food out of sight at first. Get the kids together and say something like this:

We're going outside to have a little race down to the end of the block and back. There'll be a little treat for the winner.

Now, your kids may protest a little at the idea of racing each other. The younger ones may feel at a disadvantage. When they see that they'll have to race each other on tricycles, then everybody might do a little complaining. That's OK. Just tell them that the more they complain, the more they sound like babies. The more they act like babies, the more convinced you are that a tricycle race is just perfect for them.

Anyway, go over the race rules. If you only have one trike, do it for time. If you have more than one, let the kids race each other. Have fun with this. At the end of the race, award the winner with the baby food. You might even have a spoon handy and suggest they take a bite. I would imagine your winner won't be too thrilled with the idea. That's perfect.

Now let's ask the racers a few questions. Here are a few samples:

How did you like baby food for a prize?

How did you like racing with the tricycle?

Would you like to do this again sometime?

Do you think you could have gone faster if you didn't have to use the trike?

OK, let them give you some input. We're hoping they have the opinion that they'd have been able to go faster without having to use the trike.

Yeah, the trike may be great for a little toddler, but at your age it actually slows you down. It limits you, don't you think?

A nod or a shrug for an answer may be all you get. Don't worry, they're tracking with you. They already realize that they've reacted exactly how you wanted them to with this whole thing. That can be tough for some kids to swallow. They may not like to think that they're that predictable. Anyway, you don't always need an answer from them. If they just sit there and don't answer, assume they're with you and don't want to admit it.

You would have been much faster running or, better yet, using your own bike instead of this "baby stuff" tricycle. The tricycle was never intended to be used by someone as big as you. And baby food isn't intended to be eaten by guys your age, either.

Tie It Together

What would you think if some little kid learned to pedal a trike and insisted on using it as he got older? Even when he started going to high school, he'd pedal his trike to school on nice days. He'd chain it up at the rack alongside the ten-speeds and mountain bikes of his classmates. Even when his

friends were getting their driver's licenses, this guy wouldn't give up the trike. What would you think about a guy like that?

Well, they probably think he's pretty weird to want to stick with his trike when he could drive a car instead.

Yeah, I'd say the kid was making a pretty stupid choice. What's going to happen when he wants to take a girl out on a date? It would take him forever just to get to her house. And when he gets there, where's the girl supposed to fit? What's he going to do, pull a wagon behind the trike?

Don't expect a response at this point. But if they're visualizing this kid picking up his date with a trike and a beat-up old wagon, and you get a little chuckle out of them, that's an added bonus.

It's the same way with us as Christians. We're supposed to grow and mature in our faith. If we don't, we're kind of like the boy who wouldn't give up his trike. Can you think of some areas in which a Christian may still act like a little kid instead of growing up?

Let them think about this—it may be a tough question for them. I doubt the kids have given this any real thought before. If they really look at it, it could be convicting. If they need help, you might throw out a few ideas.

Little kids are selfish. It's all about what *they* want. That's to be expected of a baby—"Wah, wah, wah, I want my bottle, I want to be

changed, I want, I want, I want. . . ." But as a growing Christian, I should be concerned about the well-being of others. I should put others first, and let God take care of me.

> Each of you should look not only to your own interests, but also to the interests of others.
>
> (Philippians 2:4)

Little kids are often inconsiderate and ungrateful. They *expect* everyone to do things for them, and you have to remind them to say "thank you" to someone. As a Christian, I should be growing in my awareness of what God is doing for me and becoming more appreciative, more thankful.

> And whatever you do, whether in word or deed, do it all in the name of the Lord Jesus, giving thanks to God the Father through him.
>
> (Colossians 3:17)

Babies don't do much for themselves. They are very *dependent* on others. Somebody has to feed them, clean up their messes, etc., etc. As a Christian, I need to grow independently strong. I can't depend on getting "fed" only when somebody spoon-feeds me at church. I need to be able to get into the Word for myself. I need to ask God to teach me as I read and study the Bible.

> Do your best to present yourself to God
> as one approved, a workman who does
> not need to be ashamed and who cor-
> rectly handles the word of truth.
>
> (2 Timothy 2:15)

> Open my eyes that I may see
>   wonderful things in your law.
>
> (Psalm 119:18)

Babies don't make terrific decisions. They
need a parent nearby to protect them from
harm. Without them, a baby might wander
into the street or tumble down the stairs. As a
Christian, you can't always have your parents
there to protect you. You'll be tempted when
we're not around. You need to make decisions on your own that God would be proud
of.

> Trust in the LORD with all your heart
>   and lean not on your own
>   understanding;
> in all your ways acknowledge him,
>   and he will make your paths straight.
>
> (Proverbs 3:5-6)

OK, we could go on with this all night. You've given them a
ton to think about; let's not overload their circuits. Wrap it up.

The kid who wouldn't give up his trike is
going to be more and more limited the older
he gets. He won't be able to do or see as much
as he would if he would move up to a car.
That will happen to us if we don't mature as

Christians. We'll limit ourselves from seeing and experiencing life as God intended we should. We'll lose out. It may even be dangerous.

Ask God to help you "grow up" as a Christian, OK?

You may want to end in prayer, maybe even have a little time of silent prayer. This would be a good time to break out a snack that the kids would love. The idea is to illustrate one more time the benefits of maturing. It sure beats baby food, doesn't it?

When the kids go to bed, you may want a little one-on-one time to see where they're at. Did today's devotions mention something that they know they need to work on? If not, that's OK. But if so, and they're open to suggestions, be ready with some practical advice, whether it's reading the Bible daily, volunteering to help someone in need, starting a journal of things to be thankful for—whatever. It's important that they begin thinking about these things.

Cut It Out!

What's the Point?

Fire up a power tool to demonstrate how God sometimes cuts things out of our lives to make us better, more effective Christians.

Things You'll Need

- A band saw, jigsaw or scroll saw
- A wide piece of 3/4" pine for cutting
- A drill and bit (optional)
- A long, skinny candle (optional)

It would be really nice to use a large, professional band saw for this, but if you can't find anybody who will let you into his workshop, a scroll saw or a jigsaw would do just as well—even a hand-held one. The key is to use a saw that will allow you to cut out some kind of shape from a piece of wood.

Here We Go

Here's the game plan: You need to decide what "shape" you want to cut out of the piece of wood. It can be anything, really, but it would be nice to pick something that will help you get your point across. Here are a couple of ideas:

1. A candleholder. Cut a circle, drill a candle-size hole and pop in a candle—presto! You've taken a hunk of wood and turned it into something useful. This would be great when it comes to an application. We're like hunks of wood. God has a master plan. He cuts away here, shapes there, until He has shaped you into the person He has designed you to be. The original hunk of wood was nice, but not nearly as well suited to bring light to a dark world as a candleholder. See how this works?

2. A sword. It's pretty easy to cut one out, and what a great way to illustrate how God wants to shape us into someone who will be more effective in the spiritual battles of life. What would you rather take into battle, a sword or a board?

Anyway, you can have fun with this. You can make a candleholder or a sword, or better yet, make one of each. That would be especially effective if you have more than one child. It helps illustrate that God has different plans for each of us. He may cut and shape our lives differently, but the end result is to make us more effective for the kingdom.

Wow, that was a long introduction, but now you've got a real feel for where we're going. After you've made all the arrangements, grab the kids and the wood and head for the workshop. You might start out with something like this:

I've got some nice wood here. I paid good money for this pine, and now I'm going to cut it up a little. Sound like a good idea?

They'll probably go along with it. That's fine. I wouldn't tell them what shape you plan to cut out. Let them figure that out as you go along.

Before using the saw, keep the kids a safe distance away. Follow the safety rules, right down to the safety goggles. Begin your cutting, then pause to get their reaction after you've lopped off a chunk of unwanted wood. You might even hold up the wood for them to see.

Well, what do you think? Is it looking better?

Who knows what you'll get for a response here. Since they don't know what you're making, they may wonder if you're actually making any improvement in the board at all. That's good. If you're cutting both the sword and the candleholder, I'd work on the candleholder first; it's harder to guess what that will be. But even if they figure out what you're making, it's no big deal.

If you're making the candleholder, don't forget to drill the hole. Be sure you've figured out the right size bit to use to drill the hole before you even start devoes. Now, pop the candle in the hole securely and light it. Let the kids inspect your little projects for a minute, and move on.

If You Want to Keep All Your Fingers

· · ·

If you aren't familiar with using the saw, be sure the owner gives you a lesson and some practice before you bring the kids into it. Tell the owner of the saw what you plan to do; he may be thrilled to do the cutting for you. And if he's not a Christian, what better way to witness than having him help with the devoes?

Tie It Together

You know, before I made the first cut, that pine board looked pretty good—for a board, that is. Did anybody wonder why I even wanted to cut it in the first place?

It doesn't really matter if they wondered or not. If they didn't wonder, that's good too. That must mean they realized you had a plan in mind. Perfect.

Well, I guess you figured out I had a plan for this wood. I didn't have a pattern drawn on the wood, but I had one in my mind. I just kept cutting off the parts of the wood that I didn't really need.

Pick up a few of the scraps you cut off and hold them up.

In order to make what I really wanted, I had to get rid of the excess wood. Let me read you some verses.

"For I know the plans I have for you," declares the LORD, "plans to prosper you and not to harm you, plans to give you hope and a future."

(Jeremiah 29:11)

For you, O God, tested us;
  you refined us like silver.

(Psalm 66:10)

Create in me a pure heart, O God,
  and renew a steadfast spirit within me.

(51:10)

Do everything without complaining or arguing, so that you may become blameless and pure, children of God without fault in a crooked and depraved generation, in which you shine like stars in the universe as you hold out the word of life.

(Philippians 2:14-16)

You know, God works on our lives sort of like I worked on this piece of wood. He has a definite plan as to the type of person He wants us to become. He works to shape our character so that we can become that person. There are things He needs to cut out of our lives so we can be more effective. What type of things might He want to get rid of in our lives?

See if they have any ideas here. If not, help them along a little.

Maybe He has to work on our pride. Maybe we need to be more humble in order to become the person He planned. Or maybe He has to work on our selfishness—it just doesn't fit in with the person He wants us to become. Or maybe He has to work on our temper a little. What other areas might He want to work on?

Give them another chance to chime in. They should definitely be seeing the point by this time.

How about our hearts? That could take a lot of work. He wants us to be more compassionate toward others. He wants us to love

Him more. See what I mean? Just like I lopped off wood that I didn't really need from this board, God works to lop off things in our lives that get in the way of our becoming the kind of people He wants us to be.

Maybe you think you're pretty satisfied with how you are right now. Maybe you don't think God will have to work on you too much. All I can say to that is, remember the board we started out with? It seemed perfectly fine. Why cut it?

You didn't know—at least, not at first— what my plans were for that board. What would be better in battle, a board or a sword? What would be better to carry in the dark, a board or a candle? It's the same way God works with us. Maybe He wants to turn you into a candleholder and carry His light to a dark world. Or maybe He wants you to be a warrior in the spiritual battles of life. Maybe He wants to turn you into a sword. Only God knows what plans He has for you. How does He cut things out of our lives? How does He shape us into the people He wants us to become?

See if they have any ideas here. If not, move on. This is an important lesson, but we don't want to overdo it. They have the idea. Let's wrap it up.

God can use all kinds of things to shape us. He uses His Word, the Bible. He also uses friends and circumstances too. He can use hard things in our lives—even tragedy—to cut things out of us that don't belong there. He uses these things to shape us into the people we need to become.

Can you think of an example in your own life or in the life of someone your kids know? This would make a nice personal touch about now.

When we run into hard times, remember that God wants to use them as an opportunity to shape us. That's a good time to pray and ask Him to do His will in your life. When you're reading your Bible, ask Him to show you areas that need to change in your life, and ask Him to help you change. Ask Him to purify you, to make you into the person He's designed you to be.

I think you've gotten the point across; time to hang it up. Why not give the things you made to the kids as a visual reminder of today's lesson? If you brought some munchies, this would be a good time to break them out.

Cleaning Up

What's the Point?

After you get your car clean on the outside, talk with your kids about how God wants to clean us up on the inside.

- A car wash
- A dirty car

The best kind of car wash for this devotional is one that allows you to stay inside the vehicle as it's being washed. If you only have the "do-it-yourself" type in the neighborhood, you can make that work too. Sure, you could wash the car at home, but going to a car wash is just more of an "event," and that may help the lesson stick in their memory a little more.

Here We Go

This one will be easy—just load the kids in the car and go through the car wash. Let the kids help you decide on the options, such as hot wax application, etc. Basically, the more you do to make the outside of the car look good, the better your lesson will be. But remember—and this is important—if the car wash is one that offers interior cleaning, you should decline. You may say something like this:

This car is going to look *so* good by the time we're done with it. Let's get the wax. We want this baby to shine.

Just before you enter the car wash, be sure all the windows and doors are shut tight. Make a big deal about it.

Are all the doors shut tight? How about the windows? We don't want to clean the inside of the car, especially while we're in it!

Now relax and enjoy the car wash. Make sure the kids are watching all the brushes and spraying water. We want them to take note of all the effort that is being made to make the car look good. When you get out of the car wash, park the car and let everyone get out to take a look at it. While not perfect, the car must look better than it did before it went in—unless one of the rollers scratched your car. In that case, watch your temper; you want the kids to remember family devotions, but not for the wrong reason!

After everyone has admired the wash job, get back in the car to make sense of this devotional. You may want to talk as you drive or stop somewhere. Anyway, say something like this:

OK, I'm sure you're wondering how the car wash ties into family devotions, right? Well, a car wash reminds me a lot of how we can be as Christians. Let me read you a couple of verses:

> Since we have these promises, dear friends, let us purify ourselves from everything that contaminates body and spirit, perfecting holiness out of reverence for God.
>
> (2 Corinthians 7:1)

> Come near to God and he will come near to you. Wash your hands, you sinners, and purify your hearts, you double-minded.
>
> (James 4:8)

> If we confess our sins, he is faithful and just and will forgive us our sins and purify us from all unrighteousness.
>
> (1 John 1:9)

> The LORD does not look at the things man looks at. Man looks at the outward appearance, but the LORD looks at the heart.
>
> (1 Samuel 16:7)

Tie It Together

When we came to the car wash, all I really cared about was how the car looked on the *outside*, but I didn't get the inside cleaned at

all. In fact, I made sure you had the windows and doors shut tight so we wouldn't get the inside cleaned by accident. That's the way we act about ourselves too. When I go to church I've showered, shaved, washed my hair and combed it nice. I try to look good.

Expect some differences of opinion here. If your kids are in their teens, your idea of "looking good" and theirs are probably football fields apart. Anyway, keep going. You're moving in for the kill.

You know what often happens? I don't pay any attention to how I look *inside*. Did you notice that one of the verses I read reminds us that God is concerned with how we look on the *inside*, not the *outside*?

OK, I had to say it, and if your kids are sharp, they'll want to know why you concern yourself so much with how they dress. If God doesn't mind, why should you? If they bring it up, you're on your own, buddy! Just roll with it and get back to the point.

God doesn't want us to "roll up the windows tight" and keep Him from cleaning inside us. He wants to clean up our bad thoughts, our selfish pride, our unforgiving spirits. He wants to make us into people who are pure and clean from the inside out. How do we let Him clean us on the inside?

Get their feedback. Work with what they give you and help them along if they need it.

We can start by inviting Him to come inside us and clean. Ask Him to show you areas in your life that need purifying. When you read your Bible or when you listen in church, you may find yourself being reminded of a part of you that needs a little cleaning. Maybe you'll remember something you need to ask forgiveness for. That one verse I read says we can depend on Him to forgive us and make us clean inside.

OK, I think you've made your point. Don't overdo it here and turn them off.

Anyway, next time you're getting all cleaned up, or you see a nice shiny car, remember to invite God to come inside and do some cleaning too.

Food Frenzy

What's the Point?

Take a trip to the grocery store to get your kids thinking about spiritual nutrition: Are they feeding on "junk food" or things of lasting value?

- A $5 bill for each kid

If you have a bunch of kids, pair them up and let them have $5 between the two of them. You could do it with $1 per person, but you'll drive home your point a lot clearer if you bite the bullet and go for $5. Then take the kids to your local grocery store for a little food frenzy. They'll have fun and learn an important lesson as well.

Here We Go

When you announce that you're going to the grocery store as part of family devoes, you may get a few weird looks. Don't let that slow you down. This will be a fun one. As you pull into the grocery store parking lot, take a minute to explain what you're planning. You might start out by saying something like this:

You're going to really enjoy this little event. I'm going to give you each $5 to spend in the grocery store on *anything* you want—as long as it's something to eat or drink. You'll have about fifteen or twenty minutes to make your choices. I want you to spend it all. What you don't spend comes back to me. When we're in the store, I don't want anybody to ask me "Can I buy this?" *You* look at the price tag and make your own decisions, OK? When you're done, go through the checkout line and pay.

Play this out however you want. If the kids aren't old enough to walk around the store on their own, you can follow them around, acting as a silent partner. If they can go on their own, you could wait by the checkout lines until they're done. It shouldn't take them long to spend the money.

Now, I expect you'll see candy, gum, soda, chips or any number of other "junk food" items. If that's the case, bite your tongue, paste on a smile and nod with approval as the kids place their goodies on the checkout conveyor. They may be making poor nutritional choices, but it will sure make teaching the devoes easier.

Hustle back home and ask each one of them to empty their bags onto the kitchen table and grab a chair. Then say something like this:

Wow, it looks like you really made a haul at the grocery store. I see a lot of soda and "snack" food here. Did anybody buy any white milk?

You want to be looking over their purchases like you figure it's there but you just don't see it. I'd expect the answer will be "no." That's perfect.

How about vegetables? Any veggies on the table?

Just give them a questioning look. Their look back should answer your question.

What about fresh fruit? Apples? Oranges? Bananas?

Do the same thing and keep the pace moving.

Anybody buy a loaf of bread? A bottle of vitamins?

I expect you'll get a lot of blank stares on this. OK, it's time to move on.

So, the way I see it, you got some really great "snack" food, but not much of anything with real nutritional value. Let me share some verses with you:

Let us therefore make every effort to do what leads to peace and to mutual edification.

(Romans 14:19)

You, my brothers, were called to be free. But do not use your freedom to indulge the sinful nature; rather, serve one another in love.

(Galatians 5:13)

Live as free men, but do not use your freedom as a cover-up for evil; live as servants of God.

(1 Peter 2:16)

Tie It Together

When I gave you the freedom to buy whatever you wanted, most of your purchases were nonnutritional things. God gives us the freedom to make all kinds of choices: how we spend our free time, how we spend our money, what type of attitude we'll have and many other options. It seems to me that pretty often the choices we make in life are similar to the choices we made in the grocery store. There's no real "nutritional" value in the choices we make. We choose things that have no lasting value. Can you give me some examples?

Give them a minute here. If they need some suggestions to prompt their thinking, here are a few: watching TV rather than

putting enough time into homework, playing video games or talking on the phone rather than taking time for personal devotions. You get the idea. Once you've gotten a little input from them, go ahead and move on. They're tracking with you.

What do you think would happen if you *always* ate the kind of food I see on the table?

They may say that they'd be thrilled. Smart-aleck kids, eh? They may not give you the answer you're fishing for, but they know the answer. That's the important thing. Kids don't always want to give us the benefit of knowing that what we're saying makes sense to them.

Well, if you always ate junk food, eventually your body would grow weaker. It wouldn't do as good a job of fighting off germs; you wouldn't be as healthy and strong as if you ate a well-balanced, nutritional diet.

OK, they get the picture by now. Wrap it up quick so you don't start boring them.

God wants us to become strong, healthy Christians. We're to be warriors for Him. He gives us the freedom to choose what we'll "feed" on—what we put in our minds, what we watch on TV, what we read, what we do with our free time. Just like it was a natural tendency to choose the "nonnutritional" foods, we often choose *spiritually* nonnutritional things as well. If we keep doing this, we'll never become all that God designed for us to be. Does this make sense to you?

Input time. If you get even the slightest nod, be thrilled.

How can we be sure to get a more balanced spiritual diet than we do now?

You may get input, you may not. Even if you don't, I'll bet they're really thinking.

At mealtime when I was a kid, I didn't get my dessert until after I ate my veggies. I think we can do the same thing with our spiritual diet. Let's make sure we have our personal devotions done before we just do whatever we want. Before you spend time talking with friends, be sure you've spent a little time talking with the Lord.

Try to be more aware of what you let into your mind. Is it nutritional? That's what the verse I read means when it uses the word "edification." When you're about to exercise your freedom in some way, ask yourself if it will make you stronger as a Christian, or if you are just filling up with spiritual "junk food"—or even spiritual "poison."

Like the one verse reminded us, we have freedom, but we should never forget we are still God's servants. Are we living like it?

Well, we could keep going, but they definitely have the picture by now. Let's not overdo it. Now you can let them enjoy their purchases. Maybe, if you're lucky, they'll even share a little with you!

Good Fires and Bad Fires

What's the Point?

A fire can do tremendous good—or tremendous damage. Here's a way to "burn" into your kids' minds that the same thing goes for our lives.

Things You'll Need

- A campfire or a grill
- A few long sticks
- A package of hot dogs and a package of hot dog rolls, or
- A bag of marshmallows
- A couple chocolate bars
- A package of graham crackers

This one can easily be done on a camping trip, but it shouldn't be that hard to do in the backyard on a cool, dry summer evening. You can use a barbecue grill for this (maybe with a few pieces of kindling to get some flames going), but if you can, go for the campfire. It's more fun for the kids. As you've probably guessed, you'll be cooking hot dogs or s'mores. Now if you don't know what a s'more is, then we'd better stop right here and tell you how to make them.

Here We Go

Get your supplies together and take the kids to your campfire spot. If you're just using the backyard grill, you might have the fire started in advance so the kids don't have to wait while you make it. When you're all set, you might start out by saying something like this:

I need you guys to find a stick so you can help me do a little cooking.

Let them find some sticks, or if you don't have any good-sized trees around, have some sticks ready in advance. Now if you're real "city slickers" and you don't even know where to find sticks, plan to pick up some ¼" dowel rods for the kids at a hardware store.

Put the hot dogs or the marshmallows on the sticks and let them start cooking. Take one marshmallow or hot dog and put it right down on the burning logs or coals. Just leave it there—you'll refer to it later. When they're done, help them put the hot dogs on the buns or the marshmallows on the graham crackers. While they're enjoying their food, start talking to them.

Good, eh? There's nothing like cooking over a fire. This is just one example of good things you can do with a fire. What are some other things?

They may tell you other things you can cook on a grill. That's OK. You also want to get them thinking beyond food. How about heat? A fire can generate life-saving heat. A fire is used to make things. Without fire we wouldn't have steel. Where would we be without steel? A fire can purify things. Have you ever "sterilized" a needle with a burning match before you used it to take a sliver from your child's foot or hand?

When you're camping, a fire can be used for protection from wild animals. Fire is sometimes used to fight a forest fire—as strange as that may seem. Fire-fighting crews will start a controlled fire to burn out a strip of trees in the path of the major forest fire. When the big fire gets there, there is nothing left to burn. It stops its unchecked spreading and the firefighters can put it out.

I'd interact with them on this subject for a couple of minutes.

OK, so we see there are plenty of *good* things a fire can be used for. Tell me about some of the *bad* things a fire can be used for.

Let 'em brainstorm here. You'll probably hear about forest fires and burning down houses. Perfect. Move on.

Yeah, a fire can be used for tremendous good, or for tremendous bad. Let me read you a couple of verses.

> But Daniel resolved not to defile himself.
>
> (Daniel 1:8)

For we are God's workmanship, created in Christ Jesus to do good works, which God prepared in advance for us to do.

(Ephesians 2:10)

Start by putting a couple of pieces of chocolate bar on half of a graham cracker. Next, slip a plump marshmallow on a stick. Heat it above the flames of the fire until it turns a golden brown and the inside is nice and gooey. Put the marshmallow on the graham cracker base with the chocolate. Take another half of a graham cracker and put it on top of the marshmallow. Put some pressure on it and slide out the stick. Voila—you have a marshmallow sandwich, also known as a "s'more."

All right, decide whether you want to cook hot dogs or s'mores over the fire, pick up your supplies and you're ready to go.

Tie It Together

Our lives can be used just like a fire. We can do a lot of good with our life. We can help others. We can provide, protect, comfort and strengthen others. That's the way it was with Daniel. He made a decision when he was young not to allow things in his life that would be wrong or destructive. His commitment paid off. Plenty of others in the Bible made the same type of decisions. Today we read their stories with a sense of awe. These people made a difference in their world.

If you want to live that type of life, it means you'll need to rely on the Lord for things like help, strength, guidance and even for forgiveness when you fail. It takes more work, but it's also more rewarding. A fire will naturally become destructive if it isn't controlled. It's the same way with us. Without letting God control us, we'll "naturally" become destructive.

Now we'll refer to that marshmallow or hot dog you left on the fire a few minutes ago. It should be extremely "well done" by now.

See that hot dog (*or marshmallow*) on the fire? Who would like to eat *that*? Nobody. It was a waste of a perfectly good hot dog (*or marshmallow*). A fire can do good things or bad things. It can cook things to perfection, and it can burn things to a crisp. We can do the same thing with our lives. Each of you has all kinds of potential—you don't want to waste it. The decision is yours, though. Daniel made a decision not to compromise, no matter what. He wanted to do the right things. He remained committed to that decision, and he became a Bible hero because of it.

Ask God to help you be like a good fire—a fire that protects and provides and comforts, not one that destroys. If that's your desire, maybe you need to make a commitment not to compromise in certain areas of your life, just like Daniel did.

Glow, Glow, Gadget

What's the Point?

A cool little invention will help you explain that if we want to become effective lights in a dark world, God may have to bend and shake us a little.

Things You'll Need

- Phosphorescent "glow sticks" (also known as "Cylume sticks"), one for each child plus one for you

There's nothing like an object lesson to get a spiritual truth across to kids. I find this especially true with my boys. Guys like gadgets, so you'll already be starting off on the right foot with devoes this week. You can get "glow sticks" at hardware or sporting goods stores. They are little plastic tubes with a couple of solutions inside. You give a shake, bend the tube hard until you feel something snap inside and give another good shake. Presto—that little baby starts glowing!

Here We Go

Wait until after dark, then grab the kids and the glow sticks. This would be ideal on a camping trip. Once you're situated in a nice dark spot, pull out one of the glow sticks. You might say something like this:

I've got one cool little invention here. This little gadget is a "glow stick." Right now it isn't doing a thing. It's pretty useless, in fact. It has potential to be *very* useful, though. All I have to do is bend it until I snap a little tube inside the stick. I shake it up and presto! The stick starts glowing. Anybody want to try it?

Go ahead and let them have the fun of making it glow. Give them a moment to take it all in, then ask them if they can figure out how it works.

There are two different chemicals in here, one in a little glass tube. When you bend the stick, the tube inside breaks, allowing the two solutions to mix together. Only then do you get the chemical reaction that makes it glow.

Now, on a bright, sunny day the glow from this stick would be barely noticeable, if at all. At night, though, it's a different story. You could read by its light. It could help you find your way in the dark. If you were lost in a cave, this would give you enough light to find your way out. Of course, when you do get out you'll be in a heap of trouble for entering the cave in the first place! But that's getting off track.

This glow stick reminds me of us. We're supposed to stand out in this dark world of ours. We're supposed to light the way for others. We're supposed to lead others to Jesus. We're supposed to help save their lives for all eternity.

Maybe you're thinking, *What can I do?* Let me read you some verses from the Bible:

> The LORD himself goes before you and will be with you; he will never leave you nor forsake you. Do not be afraid; do not be discouraged.
>
> (Deuteronomy 31:8)

> You are the light of the world. A city on a hill cannot be hidden. Neither do people light a lamp and put it under a bowl. Instead they put it on its stand, and it gives light to everyone in the house. In the same way, let your light shine before men, that they may see your good deeds and praise your Father in heaven.
>
> (Matthew 5:14-16)

> I pray that out of his glorious riches he may strengthen you with power through his Spirit in your inner being, so that Christ may dwell in your hearts through faith.
>
> (Ephesians 3:16-17)

Tie It Together

If you are a Christian, God dwells in you. His Spirit is in you. Sometimes we're like this glow stick before we bent it. We aren't really doing much. We aren't making a difference. Just like the glow stick, sometimes God has to bend us and shake us up a bit before we're willing to let the Holy Spirit really move in us. When He does, it's just like the glow stick: His light shines through us and it makes all the difference in the world.

What did Moses, Gideon and David have in common?

Get some input—I've had you talking a long time here.

All three of these Bible heroes didn't feel they could make a difference. That's the way most others looked at them too. When God bent them and shook them they ended up doing some pretty amazing things.

I have a light stick for each one of you to have some fun with. Light sticks were made to glow. It would be a waste if you never used it. In the same way, it would be a waste if you didn't let the Holy Spirit glow through you. He'll provide the power. It might involve some bending and shaking, though. That never feels good. God sometimes has to give us a problem that will "bend" us. He wants to push us just enough for us to make a decision. Will we rely on

Him and let the Spirit "glow" in us, or will we just do things our way? Are you willing to give Him a chance?

You may not think you can do much, but with God's power in a dark world, there really are no limits.

The cartoon character, Inspector Gadget, had a gadget for everything. He did all kinds of heroic deeds and helped people out with his amazing gadgets. We've got more than just a set of unique gadgets; we've got God Himself to help us. Let's get glowing for God!

Be a Straight Arrow

What's the Point?

Your kids will learn from a bow and arrow about your role as a parent—to shape their lives so they'll fly straight when they're on their own.

Things You'll Need

- A toy bow and arrow set, with at least one arrow for each child, plus one extra
- Several targets made from cardboard

To make this devotional work right, you need to warp one of the arrows in the set. Soak it in water overnight. Take it out and let it dry in a bent position for a couple of days so it ends up noticeably warped. (If the arrows in your set are not made of wood, make an arrow out of a ¼ inch wooden dowel rod and warp it.) If you can't find a toy bow and arrow set, you could make one with wooden rods and suction cups or some other type of safety padding. You can pick up dowel rods at any hardware store. Make one arrow for each child, plus a warped one.

Make about five cardboard targets with labels on them

Here We Go

Remember the story of Robin Hood? *Nobody* could shoot with a bow and arrow better than he could. He'd take careful aim and release the arrow—a bull's-eye every time! In a few moments we're going to take this bow and arrow and try a little target shooting of our own.

Did you know the Bible tells us that kids are like arrows in the hand of a warrior? Listen to this:

Sons are a heritage from the LORD,
  children a reward from him.
Like arrows in the hands of a warrior
  are sons born in one's youth.
Blessed is the man whose
  quiver is full of them.
They will not be put to shame.

(Psalm 127:3-5)

To get a better handle on what this is all about, let's try some shooting.

OK, chief—this would be a good time to move the little Indians outside. I mean, hey—let's not push your luck.

I've got some targets here. We'll set them up and see how you do.

122

Set the first target very close and let them shoot at it. If they hit a target, move it farther away and let them try again. Now pull out the warped arrow. Ask if any of them would want this one for their arrow. Let them try shooting it at a far target. Note how close they get. When you've given them enough time to shoot, gather the kids up so you can tie this lesson together in a way that will make some sense to them.

Tie It Together

So God says kids are like arrows. There's a lot to a verse like this. Let's just look at one aspect of it. As a parent, God has given me the job to help make sure you're a good "arrow"—straight and true, not warped like this one. *(Hold up warped arrow.)* He doesn't want you to be mean or selfish or disobedient. In God's eyes, that would be warped. He wants you to be honest, to love Him, to obey Him, to grow to be a warrior for Him.

As parents, we aim you at easy targets when you're young. We give you chances to obey in little ways. As you get older, we shoot for harder targets. Someday, we'll release you to fly all on your own.

Parents have no greater joy than seeing their kids shoot straight and true toward the targets God has set out for all of us in His word. These are targets like loving God with all your heart; obeying Him, trusting Him

like "Honesty," "Loving God," "Serving God," "Obeying God," "Living for God," "Faithfulness," etc. If you want, draw faces on the other side of the cardboard. When you set up the targets, position them so the kids see the faces first. Later you can flip them around so they see the attributes.

Don't Become a Target

Make sure everyone stands back when you shoot the warped arrow. Who knows where it's going to go!

and serving Him faithfully; being responsible and trustworthy as you get more and more freedom.

Turn the targets around so they see the things you wrote on the back.

Sometimes we may be hard on you. We're trying to keep you from getting warped. Remember how bad the warped arrow flew? You can never hit a target with it. We're trying to make sure you hit God's targets at the end of your flight. That's what Proverbs 22:6 is all about: "Train a child in the way he should go, and when he is old he will not turn from it."

And that's my wish for you, that you would become a "straight arrow"—flying straight and true for God.

You may want to write that verse on the arrows as a reminder.

I want each of you to take an arrow and put it in your room. Each time you see it I hope it is a little reminder to you to be a "straight arrow" for God.

Set in Concrete

What's the Point?

Want to show your kids the difference between a life built on the Rock and one built on the shifting sand of this world? Here's a "concrete" example!

Things You'll Need

- A bag of concrete mix
- A wheelbarrow or a large pail to mix it in
- A bag of sand
- Large eyebolts (the biggest you can find), one for each person (including yourself)
- A large nut for each eyebolt
- Empty plastic gallon milk containers, one for each person (including yourself)
- Water
- Small piece of wood

Cut the milk containers in half ahead of time. We'll be using the bottom as a form to pour our concrete in. You'll probably want to do this devoe where you have access to a water hose. That'll come in handy when you mix the concrete.

Here We Go

You'll have to do this devotional in two parts with enough time separating them for the concrete to set. When you're ready for part one, grab the kids and head outside. (You may want to make sure they're wearing "grubbies" and not good clothes.) You might start out saying something like this:

OK, guys. We're gonna need some help here. I have an eyebolt for each one of you and an extra one for myself. I also have these plastic milk carton bottoms for each of us. Here's what we're going to do. We're going to mix some concrete, pour it in your milk carton, put the eyebolt in it and let it set for a while.

Who wants to help mix the concrete?

Sure, let them do it. I'd suggest you control the water yourself, though. Too much water and it will get too soupy; you want a consistency like pudding. So be easy on the water, but let the kids have some fun with this.

Have them fill each plastic container with the mixture and smooth the top with a small piece of wood. (Don't fill your own container; save that for later.) Now give them each an eyebolt and nut and have them thread the nut just enough to stay on. Insert the eyebolt into the cement, threads first. Push it down deep enough so only the loop of the eyebolt remains above the cement. Finally, smooth the cement surface around the eyebolt so it looks nice.

Let them write their names in the wet cement of their masterpiece. Now, you need to give the cement plenty of time to harden before you finish the devoes. (Check the bag for hardening times.)

We're going to let these sit for a while so the cement has time to harden. Then we'll finish our devotions. There's just one more thing we have to do. I have an extra milk carton and an eyebolt. I want to make one more of these things, but instead of cement, I've got some sand here. This will be a little easier to work with.

If the sand is dry, use some water to mix in it just as if you were mixing the cement. You can have the kids do the whole thing. Have them set the eyebolt in place and you're done, for now.

After the cement has set, move on to the next part.

OK, time to finish up these devoes. Your kids have probably already figured out what they're going to see. The eyebolts in cement will stand strong, the one in the sand will pull right out. The fact that they won't be surprised is OK. It's still is a very visual reminder that they'll be more likely to remember. So anyway, get the kids together with your eyebolt creations.

Now I'm sure you can guess what's going to happen here, right?

One of your kids will probably explain exactly what you want them to see. I'd ask them to show you. Let them tug in vain at the eyebolts in the cement. Let them easily slip the one out of the sand. Don't be surprised, however, if the sand "sets up" a bit like cement; that happens with some kinds of sand. That's all the better; it will take a bit of tugging, but the sand will surely crumble away easier than the concrete!

Want to be more dramatic? Slip a rope through the bolt and attach it to the rear bumper of your car. Take a spin down the street and back. Please . . . don't go crazy on this one. Dragging it down a faster street or a highway is *not* a good idea.

Anyway, you've made your point. The eyebolt in the cement holds firm. The one in the sand does not. OK, time to move on.

Let me read you some verses from the Bible:

> Therefore, my dear brothers, stand firm. Let nothing move you. Always give yourselves fully to the work of the Lord, because you know that your labor in the Lord is not in vain.
>
> (1 Corinthians 15:58)

> The LORD is my rock, my fortress and my
>   deliverer;
> my God is my rock, in whom I take
>   refuge.
>
> (Psalm 18:2)

> Be on your guard; stand firm in the faith; be men of courage; be strong. Do everything in love.
>
> (1 Corinthians 16:13-14)

Now it is God who makes both us and you stand firm in Christ.

(2 Corinthians 1:21)

Therefore put on the full armor of God, so that when the day of evil comes, you may be able to stand your ground, and after you have done everything, to stand.

(Ephesians 6:13)

So then, brothers, stand firm and hold to the teachings we passed on to you, whether by word of mouth or by letter.

(2 Thessalonians 2:15)

You too, be patient and stand firm, because the Lord's coming is near.

(James 5:8)

Tie It Together

Many of the verses we just heard tell us to stand firm. Kind of like the eyebolts in cement. We could tug and pull, even try pulling the eyebolt out with our car. It didn't matter. The eyebolt stood firm. How do we stand firm as a Christian?

See what they say. You may be able to tie it in perfectly.

We sink ourselves into Jesus, just like we sank the eyebolt into the cement. We take time to read God's Word daily. More than just read, we need to apply what we read. See what we need to work on. Where do we fall short? We need to pray, not just before meals, but whenever we can. We simply talk to God.

One verse we read describes God as our Rock. He doesn't change. Just like we anchored the eyebolt in the cement, we anchor ourselves in Him. Our faith is strengthened as a result. You see, everybody anchors themselves somewhere. If you don't anchor yourself to the Rock, where do you anchor yourself?

Tough question, but ask it anyway. See if they come up with an answer.

If you aren't anchoring yourself in God, you're anchoring yourself in the world. That may be in relationships with others. It may be in sports. It could be in a lot of things. A lot of people anchor themselves in their jobs when they get older. Many depend on their money or other people.

I'm not saying all these things are bad. It's just that they're like sand—they shift and change. Ultimately they aren't enough to help you stand firm in a world that is full of evil.

This whole cement thing is getting pretty heavy. If the kids seem to be really into the discussion, keep it going. You can do that by asking them questions, or by asking them if they have questions. Otherwise, we need to wrap it up.

There's a pretty familiar passage in the Bible that you'll recognize when I read it. It's the story of the wise man who built his house on the rock as contrasted with the foolish man who built on the sand. Listen to this:

Read Matthew 7:24-27.

Sinking yourself into a world that is changing won't help you when you really need it, any more than the foolish man's house was able to protect him. You need to be set in concrete—in the Rock, the One who does not change. It took more time and effort to mix the cement than it did the sand. The big difference is that the sand didn't hold. It takes some effort to read your Bible and to give God the things that need to change in your life. It takes an effort to pray, especially for others. But that's the only way to anchor yourself in the Rock. He can help you stand firm when others are being swept away with the world.

I'd love to keep going and going. I try to avoid preaching, but I may be getting close on this one! Play it by ear with your group. As you wind this one down, you might ask them what changes they intend to make, if any, based on what you talked about today. If they want to change, but they're not sure how, pray with them about it. The main thing is that they change their thinking on the importance of anchoring themselves in the Rock. Help them find some practical ways they can read the Bible more and actively apply it.

Secret Weapon

What's the Point?

This object lesson explains how the cross of Christ shows that God is always in control—even when things look really bad.

Things You'll Need

- A piece of wood, about 1" thick by 3" wide and about four feet long
- Screws or nails

You need to make a wooden sword from this piece of wood. Don't panic—something simple will work just fine. Remember how you made 'em as a kid? Just cut off about six inches and screw or nail it perpendicular to the other piece about six inches from one end. Sharpen the end, and you've got yourself a sword. Of course, if you're skilled at woodworking, you may want to make an even better-looking sword.

Dig a hole in the yard somewhere and bury the tip of the sword so it stands upright and looks like a cross. If you got carried away and made the sword with too much detail like I did, even if you bury the sharp end they'll still know it's a sword. I ended up wrapping the grip and cross guard part of the sword with

Here We Go

Be sure the sword is buried and disguised to look like a cross, not a sword. Get the kids outside and start out with something like this:

Guys, today we're going to talk a little about what Jesus did for us on the cross. I've made this little cross you see here to give us something to look at while we talk about it. What do you think was going on in the minds of the disciples and Mary when Jesus was nailed to the cross?

Let them give their thoughts. If you're hearing things like, "they felt discouraged, helpless, hopeless, afraid," that's good. If they're stuck, help them out a little.

Yeah, I'm sure the disciples felt like they had been defeated by the Pharisees and the forces of evil. How do you think the Pharisees felt?

They'll probably say that the Pharisees felt pretty happy. So far so good.

Yeah, the Pharisees must have felt that they'd won the battle. They outsmarted Jesus. They defeated Him. They outsmarted the crowd into demanding His execution. They outsmarted the Romans into helping the whole process along. They had to feel like they finally had everything back under their control.

Of course, they made one little miscalculation. The disciples did too, for that matter. What was that little miscalculation? Any ideas?

If you get some input, great. If all you're getting is blank stares and shoulder shrugs, move on.

They didn't know something Jesus knew. They didn't know they were playing right into His hands. When Jesus drew His last breath on the cross, the Pharisees thought they'd won. In reality, it was Jesus who won the victory. Let me read you some verses:

> This grace was given us in Christ Jesus before the beginning of time, but it has now been revealed through the appearing of our Savior, Christ Jesus, who has destroyed death and has brought life and immortality to light through the gospel.
>
> (2 Timothy 1:9-10)

> Since the children have flesh and blood, he too shared in their humanity so that by his death he might destroy him who holds the power of death—that is, the devil— and free those who all their lives were held in slavery by their fear of death.
>
> (Hebrews 2:14-15)

> "For my thoughts are not your thoughts, neither are your ways my ways," declares the LORD.
>
> (Isaiah 55:8)

aluminum foil nice and thick. It looked like a chunky silver cross when the kids saw it.

Tie It Together

By dying on the cross, Jesus made it possible for each of us to be rescued, to be saved. The Pharisees thought Jesus was a "has-been," but He was a hero. People belittled His power. They said He couldn't even save Himself. In reality, He saved the world. He changed history. From that point on, the devil and his demons had to change their strategy. Jesus has defeated the evil powers, so now their goal is to keep people from knowing the truth. Jesus also defeated death. Those of us who are saved know that death has no real power over us. It simply ushers us into eternal life with Jesus.

Now grab the "cross" by its top (the handle of the sword). You might say something like this:

When I think of the cross, I think of it more as a weapon.

Pull out the sword with all the dramatic flair of a Hollywood hero.

I think of it as a sword—a sword that Jesus used to defeat the Pharisees, for sure. But more importantly, a sword He used to defeat the power of death and the devil and his demons.

The kids may want to see the sword. Hand it over to them. If their mind is focused on getting it, they won't be listening to you. After a minute or two, move on to an application a little closer to home.

Remember how we talked about the way the disciples must have felt when Jesus died on the cross? How do you think they would have felt if they knew what Jesus was *really* doing? How would they have felt if they realized Jesus had just defeated the devil? How would they have felt if they knew their Lord had just saved the world?

Let them think about this. They'll probably say the disciples would have been happy. They may have cheered. OK, now they're ready for you to move in for the final point.

The disciples were scared, discouraged, etc., because they didn't realize what Jesus was *really* up to. Did you ever stop to think that Jesus operates the same way today? What we may consider to be a defeat may really be a victory by the time Jesus gets through with it! We can't possibly know what Jesus has planned. Who would ever have guessed the secret of the cross when Jesus was on it? Who would have guessed He was going to do all those amazing things?

Sometimes we go through things that make us worried or even scared. Everything may seem to be going wrong. Some situation has gone out of control and maybe we end up feeling like a big loser. After seeing how the disciples felt when Jesus died, what should you and I think about when we go through scary or discouraging times?

OK, time to see if they got it or not. We don't want to beat them over the head with the lesson. It's an important concept to know, but tough to put into practice. This lesson is just one small step toward that end. Let's wrap it up.

The thing is, we can't possibly guess what God is *really* doing behind the scenes. We can trust Him, though. God is in control. He wants us to trust Him even when we might be scared or discouraged, or when we feel like a loser.

That's one of the cool secrets of the cross. Jesus' enemies thought they'd beat Him. That's the way it looked. They just didn't realize that Jesus was using the cross like a sword to defeat them all. He had just saved the world!

You may want to give the sword to one of the kids to put in the corner of their room as a reminder to them about the truth of this devotional. If you're anything like me, you could use the reminder yourself sometimes!

Time to Burn

What's the Point?

Try this hot idea: using a torch to impress on your kids the importance of using time wisely!

Things You'll Need

- A small propane torch
- A variety of small flammable objects you can "torch"
- A couple of dollar bills (don't worry, we won't burn them!)
- A garden hose or a bucket of water—just in case

You can pick up a propane torch at your local hardware store pretty inexpensively. If this is totally out of the question, you can use a lighter. I gotta tell you, though, the torch will be more dramatic and will hold the kids' attention better.

As you collect things to "torch," use your imagination. Paper or cardboard toys work pretty well. Food items are also great to use. The kids will get a real kick out of "toasting" bread with a torch. How about hot dogs, marshmallows or a banana? A plas-

Here We Go

Grab your torch along with the things you plan to burn and head outside with the kids. Don't even think about doing this inside. I'd get far from anything you wouldn't like to see burned. It may be a bit dangerous for your kids to be leaning over the stuff they are burning up, so find a large rock, a metal trash can or something else (as long as it's not flammable) on which to set the objects that you're going to burn. And of course, have the garden hose or a bucket of water close by.

Gather the kids around and show them the torch. If your kids are older, get them involved. Pass the torch around (before you light it). You might say something like this:

OK, guys. I've got some things in this bag that we're going to toast with this torch.

They should be excited just thinking about this. You may want to go over a few safety rules, such as: always point the torch away from yourself and others; never touch the end of the torch, even if it's off (it gets very hot); turn off the torch before handing it to someone else. You may be able to come up with a few rules of your own.

Pull the things you're going to torch out of the bag and say:

Which one of these do we torch first?

Whatever they want works for this lesson. Save the milk carton of water for the end just in case you need to put out a small fire. Now, if you really want this lesson to stick in their minds, let *them* do the burning. I know, I know—this is a stretch for you.

You're afraid someone will get hurt, right? (And maybe there's a little part of you that wants to have all the fun!) I went through the same thing. Go ahead, let them do it—under your careful supervision, of course. Let everyone have a turn. It's OK to take your time here. The kids won't forget the fun they had with the torch. And they won't forget the lesson, either.

After all the stuff has been burned, take charge of the torch and get their attention. Pull a couple of bucks from your pocket and say something like this:

What would you think about burning some money?

Between letting them play with the torch and now suggesting they burn money, your kids may begin to wonder about you. Get their reaction to the idea anyway. Think of some other things that would be very valuable to them and ask if they'd like to try torching those items. It could be favorite toys, a baseball mitt, a CD player, etc. Get their reaction to these ideas. While they find it fun to burn worthless things, you want them to totally dislike the idea of burning anything valuable to them.

Let me share some Bible verses with you:

A sluggard does not plow in season;
so at harvest time he looks but finds
nothing.

(Proverbs 20:4)

Be very careful, then, how you live—not as unwise but as wise, making the most of every opportunity, because the days are evil.

(Ephesians 5:15-16)

tic milk carton filled with water is great. You torch a hole through it and the water shoots out.

OK, I know what you're thinking. This lesson sounds like you're teaching the kids to play with fire. I realize that's a big "no-no," so think of it this way: You're not really playing, although you will have fun. You're using the torch to teach a lesson. There's a big difference.

To Avoid a Hospital Bill . . .

Have some fun with this, but don't burn anything that may flare up or give off toxic smoke. (You don't want to be finishing devoes in the emergency room!)

Tie It Together

We've seen that "torching" things can really be a lot of fun, provided we torch the *right* things. Torching money or things that are really valuable would be crazy.

There is something that God has given us; it's extremely valuable, and we've *all* been guilty of "torching" it. The verses I just read should give you a hint. Any idea of what I'm talking about?

See what they say here. They may come up with some pretty good things that we haven't thought of. Maybe you can work them in. Otherwise, say something like this:

Yeah, God has given us a lot of valuable things. The one I'd like us to think about for a few minutes is *time*. Time is much more valuable than money. Ask a millionaire dying of cancer. He'd gladly trade his money for more time to live. Money won't do him any good when he's dead.

Time is so valuable and God has given the same twenty-four hours every day to each of us. The question is, what do we *do* with the time God has given us? Would He be happy with how we spend our time? Would He look at what we do as a waste of time?

See if you can get them to open up and give you some of their thoughts right now.

When we waste time, when we don't use it wisely, when we don't use time in ways that please God, it's like we're torching something very valuable. Can you imagine burning up your birthday presents before you even opened them? That's insane. We do something just as crazy when we waste time. We burn up the time we waste; we can never get it back. Whatever God had planned for us to do in that time is gone.

What are some things we do that God might consider a waste of time?

Get their input. You may get some real eye-opening answers here. They may mention things like too much TV or video games or any number of things. The more things *they* bring up, the less "preaching" you should do. Just listen. Nod your head if they bring up a good one. Let the Holy Spirit work. Be careful not to go too long.

What are some things that God might think are a wise use of the valuable gift of time He has given us?

Again, let them talk. You want to keep from giving input yourself unless the kids are silent. Certainly things like reading their Bible and praying should come up. You also want to come up with creative alternatives to the time spent watching TV, etc. If all they come up with are "work"-type suggestions, remind them that, in moderation, recreation and relaxation are also a worthwhile use of one's time.

I think we all need to work on making better use of our time. Where do you plan to start?

Yep, we want each of them to come to some kind of personal commitment. Tell them that you are willing to help them in any way you can. One way you might suggest is accountability. That will take some work, but it's worth it. Have them write down what changes they plan to make. Then—tactfully—ask how they're doing with it from time to time. Just be sure not to use this as a club against them: "I thought you were going to stop wasting time on computer games! You've been playing around for an hour on this thing . . . blah, blah, blah." Say something like that and they may never open up to you again!

If you're really brave, you may want to admit to your kids what things *you* waste time on, and ask them to keep you accountable. Trust me, they'll remember to do it!

When you're done, remind the kids that the torch is not for them to use without you. I'd also play it extra safe with the items you burned. Douse them thoroughly with water before you throw them out.

By the way, I think the kids enjoyed this one. I'll bet you did, too. See, devoes *can* be fun!

Where Am I?

What's the Point?

Take the kids on a "mystery ride" to illustrate how we can have confidence in God—even though we may be totally confused about where we are.

Things You'll Need

- Your car
- A blindfold for each kid
- A pencil and paper for each kid

Do this one at night, using your car. Map out a route that includes several stops in places that are close to home, but hard to recognize, such as: behind the grocery store, between the dumpster and a stack of skids; in the maze of an industrial park; the parking garage of a hospital or hotel. Look for places that the kids may not recognize when they take off their blindfolds.

Here We Go

Get your route all planned (let's face it, a dry run on your own would be smart, but if you're a guy like me, you'll probably settle for mapping it out in your head), then get the blindfolds and get the kids. You might open with something like this:

OK, everybody. I'm ready for our devoes, but I'll need you to get in the car first. When you get there, buckle in and put on a blindfold. I want it good and tight—no cheating! As soon as everyone is ready, we're going to take a little drive.

I'm going to make a few stops along the way. When I do, I'll ask you to take off your blindfold, look around and write down where you think we are.

Make sure all the blindfolds are on securely before you pull out. Drive around the block a few times to get them disoriented, then proceed to your first stop. Ideally, you should select places where the kids can stay in the car and just look out the window. Put the car in park and say something like this:

OK, in a minute I'm going to let you take off the blindfold. I'll give you ten seconds to take a quick look around and another ten seconds to write down exactly where you think we are. Don't say it out loud—write it down. Ready? Take off the blindfold!

When the time is up, make sure they get those blindfolds back on. Hopefully, the kids will be confused by their surroundings in at least one or more of the spots you pick. Proceed to each of the other stops and follow the same pattern as you did the first time.

A word to the wise here—drive carefully! Resist the temptation to drive like a maniac just to confuse the kids more. You really don't want to draw any unnecessary attention to yourself from other drivers. I mean, think about it: Somebody sees you driving like an idiot and glances over to see if you look as nutty as you drive. That's when they see the kids with the blindfolds on! They put two and two together and figure you're a good parent leading family devotions? I don't think so! They're going to pick up their cell phone and the next thing you know, you're surrounded by some very intense police officers. The kids will pull down their blindfolds just in time to see Dad being frisked. If you have teenagers, don't count on them to back up your story. I'm picturing a family devotional event that the kids will *never* forget. So drive sensibly, OK?

When you've made your last stop, have them leave their blind-folds on as you head to a fast-food place or an ice cream stand. They'll take off their blindfolds and—surprise! Treats for everyone!

As they're eating their snack, explain where you were on each of the stops. They can look at their sheets to see how many spots they were able to figure out correctly. Next, ask them some questions, such as:

- How many stops were you able to guess correctly?
- Was there any stop at which you took off the blindfold and felt totally confused as to where you were?

- Did you ever feel a sense of panic, like, "Hey—I'm lost!"?
- Did you get scared at any point?

Get their input here.

Did you think about jumping out of the car and trying to find your way home on your own?

They should be answering "No" to these last few questions, we hope!

Why didn't you get scared or panic?

Hopefully they'll say something like, "You were driving. You knew where you were going," etc. These questions might seem a little lame, but they're important. They set up the opportunity to compare this little field trip with life. Time to share some Scripture.

Let me read a Bible passage to you:

Where can I go from your Spirit?
   Where can I flee from your presence?
If I go up to the heavens, you are there;
   if I make my bed in the depths, you are
      there.
If I rise on the wings of the dawn,
   if I settle on the far side of the sea,
even there your hand will guide me,
   your right hand will hold me fast.

(Psalm 139:7-10)

Tie It Together

When you were riding in the car with the blindfold on, you probably didn't know ex-

actly where we were. When we stopped
and I had you pull off the blindfolds, even
then you weren't always entirely sure. But
nobody worried too much about it because
you trusted me. Now, if you were driving, especially if you had a blindfold on, you
might have reason to be scared! But you
could relax because I knew where we were
and I was driving.

God wants us to relax with Him too. Sometimes we worry a lot more than we should.
We panic sometimes when we find ourselves
in situations we've never been in before. We
get confused as to where we're going or
where we are. We get scared because we feel
lost and don't know where to go.

We forget that we don't have to be
scared, any more than you were scared
when you were blindfolded. God *always*
knows where we are. That's what those
verses tell us. He's not lost—He's at the
steering wheel. He'll take us where we need
to go. You don't have to worry about things.
Just as I brought you to all those crazy
places to teach you this lesson, God sometimes brings us to places in our life that will
teach us lessons too.

What are some things that you're worried about?

You can rephrase that question a couple of different ways: "What types of things do you tend to worry about?" Or maybe, "What types of things do kids your age worry about?" It may also help them open up if you admit to some of the things *you* worry about. (Don't be afraid that such a confession will damage your reputation—I gave up trying to be "Superdad" a long time ago!)

Anyway, this is a good time to find out what your kids are really concerned about—what really rattles their cages. You may learn a lot from this question. If you get some real specific input from them, great. You may want to use it as you end your devoes. Otherwise, you may want to close your time with something like this:

So remember, God always knows where you are. Don't try to sit in the driver's seat. Don't try to get out of the car and find your own way. Trust God and ask Him to take you where He knows you need to go.

The truth is, this is a pretty good reminder for parents too. We've got to work on that. If we can't trust God, then why bother with family devotions at all? Our faith isn't worth passing on if it doesn't work for us. I know it isn't easy. Let's ask God to help us with that too, OK?

Other Books
by Tim Shoemaker

Tried and True Job

Wearing the Mask